A Banqueter's Guide to the All-Night Soup Kitchen of the Kingdom of God

Patrick T. McCormick

LITURGICAL PRESS

Collegeville, Minnesota

www.litpress.org

Cover design by David Manahan, O.S.B. Photo courtesy of Neville Hughs and Holy Apostles Church, New York City.

Scripture quotations are from *New Revised Standard Version Bible: Catholic Edition,* copyright 1989, 1993, Division of Christian Education of the National Council of the Churches of Christ in the United States of America. Used by permission. All rights reserved.

Although not quoted, the author gratefully acknowledges his use of The Oxford Study Bible: Revised English Bible with the Apocrypha, ed. M. Jack Suggs, Katherine Doob Sakenfeld, and James R. Mueller (New York: Oxford University Press, © 1992).

6　　　　7　　　　8

Library of Congress Control Number: 2003105714

ISBN 0-8146-2955-5

To Guay,
eucharistō poli

Contents

"Do This in Memory of Me"

Jesus directs this command to his disciples at the Last Supper, and the Church has lodged it in the heart of every eucharistic prayer (see 1 Cor 11:24). Indeed, for two thousand years Christians have remembered and followed this instruction by celebrating the Eucharist. In this memorial meal we remember Christ's passion, death, and resurrection. Every time we gather in the Eucharist we celebrate an *anamnesis* or remembrance of the one who left this command. And this remembrance is far more than just a calling to mind, for in the Eucharist we are "re-membered" to Christ. In the Eucharist, Christ becomes radically present to us, and we (the Church) celebrate our identity as the Body of Christ and join in the mystery of the Cross and Resurrection.

But Christians have also long known that obeying the command to "do this in memory of me" means much more than just celebrating the Eucharist. Or, better yet, that celebrating the Eucharist as a remembrance of Christ means practicing God's justice towards neighbors, strangers, and enemies alike. For in the Eucharist we are called to re-member ourselves to the one who was anointed "to bring good news to the poor. He has sent me to proclaim release to the captives and recovery of sight to the blind, to let the oppressed go free" (Luke 4:18). In the Eucharist we celebrate a remembrance of the one who called us to show hospitality to the poor, to welcome sinners and outcasts as friends, and to become the servants of the lowly and downtrodden. In this *anamnesis* we honor the dangerous memory of the one who took "the form of a slave," (Phil 2:7) who sided with the world's poor and oppressed and who became one of its despised, disappeared, and executed scapegoats. In this memorial we remember the one who told us that every time we forget the hungry, the naked, the homeless, the sick, or the imprisoned we forget him (see Matt 25:31-46).

And in the Eucharist we remember things not yet seen. We celebrate a remembrance of a reign shot through with God's mercy and justice, a topsy turvy world where the high and mighty have been cast down, and where the outcasts and beggars have been invited to a wedding feast of unimaginable bounty. We remember a banquet where the poor are honored guests; where the widowed, orphans, and aliens are served sumptuous portions; where slaves and servants are waited upon by kings and lords; where every wall between masters and slaves, males and females, rich and poor has been torn down.

Celebrating this remembrance, then, means becoming a community that practices God's justice, a justice that shows compassion to the poor, forgiveness to sinners, and love to enemies. Celebrating the Eucharist in memory of Christ means that we must stand in solidarity with all the impoverished, marginalized, oppressed, and abused; that we must confront, resist, and dismantle every practice, structure, and system that ignores the cries of the poor or grinds down the world's widowed, orphaned, and alienated. Remembering Christ in the Eucharist means re-membering ourselves to all the nobodies and victims being ignored by or trampled underneath our various economic, political, social, and religious structures. Celebrating a remembrance of Christ means never forgetting the faces, cries, and sufferings of the hungry, poor, displaced, discouraged, disenfranchised, and desperate millions standing outside our banquet halls.

The early Christians understood that celebrating the Eucharist and imitating God's justice were overlapping practices. The church of Acts grasped that any community that gathered to remember Christ in "the breaking of the bread" also needed to share that bread with the poor and the hungry, and to make room at their tables and in their homes for all beggars and outcasts. Paul reprimanded the rich Christians of the church in Corinth for failing to share their food and bounty with the poor, and informed them that they were clearly not celebrating the Lord's Supper when they behaved in this manner (1 Cor 11:18-22). Later Christians stressed the connection between the Eucharist and justice by introducing a collection for the poor to be taken up during every celebration, and in recent times Christians like

Virgil Michel, Dorothy Day, and Monika Hellwig have recovered this connection between remembering Christ in the Eucharist and re-membering the poor and oppressed in our daily lives.

This is a book about the Eucharist and justice, about the connection between re-membering ourselves to Christ and re-membering ourselves to the poor, oppressed, marginalized, executed, and forgotten. In this book I argue that the Eucharist is a feast of remembrance, an *anamnesis* that opens us up to the dangerous memories of a Christ who stands with, embraces, and becomes one of the poor—who takes on the mortal and frail flesh of the hungry, sick, naked, homeless, dispossessed, and disappeared. In the Eucharist we are called to remember all the blessings we have received from God and all the ways in which neighbors, strangers, even enemies—indeed all other creatures—are part of this blessing. We are also called to remember all the ties and duties that bind us to others. Injustice begins with forgetting, with forgetting the faces and cries of the poor. In the Eucharist we are called to re-member ourselves to those we have forgotten, for we cannot remember Christ and forget the poor.

By calling us to remember Christ and to remember our duties to the poor the Eucharist functions as a kind of school for manners, teaching us God's justice by training us in Jesus' table manners. In this memorial meal we remember, proclaim, and practice the radical table fellowship of Jesus and the etiquette of God's heavenly banquet. In this *anamnesis* we re-member ourselves to the Body of Christ, a body that is broken, tortured, oppressed, and ravaged by injustice and violence.

To enkindle our eucharistic memory of the poor, I have turned to four metaphors Christians have long used to speak about the Eucharist: bread, table, body, and sacrifice. I explore the ways in which thinking about the Eucharist as bread or food awakens us to our own identity as hungry eaters and awakens us to our ties to all the world's hungry and malnourished—as well as to all those who prepare, provide, and become our daily bread. We are also connected to (and divided from) many of the world's poor and oppressed by our various tables, and sitting down at the eucharistic table evokes the memory of the one who calls us to practice a radically new table fellowship. At the eucharistic table we remember Jesus instructing us to invite beggars and outcasts to our banquets, and to get up and wash the feet of servants. So too, we remember in the Eucharist that we are all part of the Body of Christ, and that being part of this body means standing with and caring for all the world's nobodies. Finally, in this memorial of Christ's sacrifice we are reminded of our vocation to reject every sort of scapegoating and to take up the yoke of every victim of injustice, oppression, and violence.

Obeying the command to "do this in memory of me" means celebrating the Eucharist in ways that re-member us to the one who identified with all the world's forgotten. It means celebrating a dangerous memory that will transform us into the sort of community that practices Jesus' table manners and remembers the beggars' banquet to which he summoned us. It means never forgetting that this bread, table, body, and sacrifice call us to "to do justice, and to love kindness, and to walk humbly with your God" (Mic 6:8).

There are many people to give thanks to *(eucharisteō)* for this book. My parents, Bill and Barbara McCormick, were my first teachers in eucharistic table manners, and no doubt my best. For nearly three decades the Philadelphia Province of the Vincentians schooled and formed me in a eucharistic ethic based on St. Vincent DePaul's call to "preach the good news to the poor," forever driving home the point that celebrating the Eucharist and doing justice were two practices that needed to go hand in hand. And over the past decade my family and I have experienced and benefited from the extraordinary eucharistic hospitality of Linda Kobe Smith and St. Ann's Parish in Spokane, Washington. It is not possible to give adequate thanks to these people.

I would also like to acknowledge the influence and contribution of Monika Hellwig's wonderful book, *The Eucharist and the Hunger of the World* (rev. ed. [Kansas City, Mo.: Sheed & Ward, 1992]), which I read many years ago in graduate school and which has had a lasting impact on my imagination. And I would like to say a word of thanks to my colleague James Dallen, who pointed me to a number of fine resources in preparing this text, and to Kevin Eiler, a graduate student at Gonzaga, whose research and close reading saved me countless hours of work.

My final word of thanks goes to my wife Guay, who is a blessing to me in countless ways—and who urged me for years to write this book—and who patiently supported me (and listened to my ideas and complaints) through the sabbatical year during which it was written.

Chapter One

Take and Eat

A Sacrament of Eating and Drinking

"Take this, all of you, and *eat* it. . . . Take this, all of you, and *drink* it." Jesus gives these commands to his disciples at the Last Supper, and we hear them every Sunday.[1] Lodged in the heart of each eucharistic prayer, they remind us that Christianity's central sacrament is a ritual about eating and drinking, hunger and thirst, feeding and being fed. That is not all the Eucharist is about. But we miss something important when we forget this dimension or ignore its moral implications.

I first heard these commands as a fourth grader serving Mass. Listening for a signal to ring the bells at the consecration, I knew we were getting close when the priest whispered in Latin, *"Accipite, et* manducate *ex hoc omnes."* A few moments later I prepared to shake the hand bells again when he prayed, *"Accipite et* bibite *ex eo omnes."*

In those pre-Vatican II days, when I was preparing for confirmation by memorizing the *Baltimore Catechism,* I didn't have any trouble believing that the wafer in the priest's hands was being transformed into the Body of Christ. But I never thought of the thin little host he put on our tongues as food. Even in an age when the sandwich in my Roy Rogers lunchbox was made with snowy white Wonder Bread, bleached of most of its nutritional value, those half-dollar-sized wafers passed out at the communion rail seemed far too anemic to be real bread.

1

Indeed, if I made any connection back then between the Eucharist and food, it was a link between Mass and *not* eating. In the late '50s and early '60s we were ordered to fast for three hours before receiving Communion, and on Sunday mornings this usually meant not having anything to eat until we got home from the ten o'clock Mass. This eucharistic fast whetted my appetite for Sunday brunch, but it didn't make me more aware of the fact that the Eucharist was about eating and drinking.

We did learn in our catechisms that the bread and wine on the altar were the "matter" or what we might call the "stuff" of the Eucharist, and Church law required that we approach the altar and eat of this sacred food at least once a year. Still, most of us considered this *panis angelicus* (bread of the angels) as purely spiritual nutrition, a high octane but ethereal manna that filled our souls with sanctifying grace and supplied us with all the weekly nutrients required for eternal salvation. We rarely asked ourselves what it meant to celebrate a sacrament centered around the simple bodily act of eating. And we hardly ever wondered about the moral implications of celebrating this sacrament of eating and drinking in a world where so many were starving or malnourished—and where we Americans were gobbling up a huge portion of the world's resources. The otherworldly fare we were served at the Communion rail reminded us that we did not live by bread alone, but we did not often ask what eating this wafer meant about our ties to those who couldn't get their daily bread.

At our dinner tables at home we did make some connections between eating and our ties to others. During grace before supper we would bow our heads and thank God for the food in front of us, acknowledging our dependence on the Creator's generosity, though not usually on the labor of those who brought this food to our plates. And when we shied away from eating our brussels sprouts and lima beans our parents would remind us of the starving children in China or Armenia, so that the ghosts of the hungry were present at our tables at least as a prod to eat our vegetables.

At Thanksgiving and Christmas we often made a connection between our big meals at home and our obligations to the hungry folks down at the local mission or shelter. We'd have food drives at school and bring in canned and dry goods to give to poor folks who couldn't afford a turkey and all the trimmings.

But standing in the communion line we rarely asked ourselves what it meant to be an eater, or what moral duties eating and drinking created in us toward other eaters, the hungry, those who fed us, those who were our food, or those for whom we would someday be food. I cannot remember a single childhood sermon making a connection between the bread on our altars and the hunger in the bellies of the poor, or suggesting that in the Eucharist we were celebrating a banquet of beggars connecting us to the hungry everywhere. Indeed, I've often thought it curious that *Stone Soup*—Marcia Brown's prizewinning tale about villagers who create a feast by sharing—was my favorite children's book (read to me by Captain Kangaroo), and yet I never made the connection between that story and the miracle of the loaves and fishes—recorded in all four Gospels and remembered in the Eucharist. Perhaps that's because I never heard a homilist suggest that a miraculous sharing might have helped fill up those twelve baskets of leftovers.

Back then we thought of Mass mostly as an "unbloody sacrifice" and focused our attention on the consecration of the bread and wine into the Body and Blood of Christ. So we tended to overlook the fact that in the Eucharist we were celebrating a meal, a meal that invoked not just the memory of the Last Supper, but of Jesus' feeding the multitudes with a few loaves of shared bread, and of early Christians sharing their food with the poor and hungry. We forgot that eating the bread being blessed, broken, and distributed by our priest made us companions (from the Latin for sharing bread with) with the hungry Hebrews being fed manna in the wilderness, and with all the beggars and outcasts gathered around the heavenly banquet table. And we forgot that eating and drinking at the Eucharist put us at table with hungry eaters everywhere and with all those whose flesh and sweat had gone into our daily bread.

In many ways this forgetfulness, this failure of our sacramental and moral imagination, kept our eucharistic manna from being much more than pablum for us, and we often went home with the ethical implications of the Bread of Life undigested in our hearts. All too regularly we left the communion rail unaware of our identity as hungry eaters and untroubled by the gap between this sacrament of eating and drinking and what we were doing in the world. In an era when a fifth of the planet was hungry and the people of the United States were becoming the most voracious and unthinking consumers of all of creation's bounty, we were going to the Eucharist every Sunday and never wondering what it meant to eat and drink.

Recently, however, a growing chorus of voices in the Church has reminded us that the bread and wine we eat and drink in the Eucharist makes moral demands upon us and that this meal has something to say about all the other meals in our lives—and all the meals that so many of our neighbors go without.[2] These authors have also reminded us that if (as Paul warns the Corinthians) we are to avoid eating the Lord's Supper unworthily, we will need to share our food with the hungry and honor those whose labor and bodies produce our daily bread. For in the Eucharist we celebrate the death and resurrection of Christ within the setting of a meal, a meal in which food and drink are sacraments of our need and God's grace. To eat this meal worthily— to accept this bread that has been blessed, broken, and shared with us—we must be willing to bless, break, and share our bread with others who are hungry, and give thanks and honor to those who bring our daily bread to our tables.

The Eucharist, then, calls us to recognize ourselves as eaters, to look at what we are doing when we eat, and to ask how this food and drink tie us to God, the hungry, and all those people and creatures whose labor and bodies produce our meals. For if this sacrament of eating and drinking is to be celebrated worthily in a world where plenty and hunger are uneasy neighbors, if it is to be more than an empty ritual or a scandal to the poor, then this bread and wine must be a leaven in our conscience, awakening us to Jesus' command to his disciples, "You give them something to eat" (Luke 9:13).

This chapter, then, examines the moral implications of the Eucharist *as* food, asking what it means for us to celebrate a sacrament about eating and drinking in a nation—and world—where the beggar Lazarus continues to starve just outside our gates, and what the Eucharist demands of us when it awakens us to our identity as hungry eaters. We begin by asking what it means to be an eater and what might be involved in eating consciously. Then we look at some symptoms of contemporary America's dis-ease with food and four ways in which we eat unconsciously (and thus unjustly and unworthily). Finally, we will see how the Eucharist calls and empowers us to be conscious eaters, and what sort of leaven a eucharistic community is called to be in a hungry world.

The Meaning of Eating and Drinking:
Recognizing Ourselves as Hungry Eaters

Food and Hunger

We are eaters, hungry eaters who need food to live, and we never stop needing it. Every living organism on the planet, from the sperm whale to the single-celled amoeba, needs a steady supply of food to stay alive. We don't all read, talk, walk, fly, crawl, or swim, and we don't all have stomachs, mouths, tongues, or teeth, but in one way or another we all need to eat. Each of us has to take in some carbon-based material from our environment and metabolize it—making it a part of ourselves and providing us with the energy and material we need to grow, work, rest, repair or reproduce ourselves, and stay alive. Plants and some bacteria are called "autotrophic" because they can make their own food, using photosynthesis to take carbon dioxide out of the air and turn it into nutrition. The rest of us are "hetero-trophic" because we get our nourishment and carbon by consuming other organisms. But either way, we all need food.

An average-sized adult human male needs between 2,300 and 3,700 calories per day (depending on how active he is) while a woman requires about 1,800 to 2,400 calories per day. Whether we are dining on caviar and escargot at a lovely little bistro, or a chili dog and chips at the ball park, we get these calories from eating carbohydrates, proteins, and/or fats. If we take in more food than needed, the excess is stored as body fat, and if we eat less than required to maintain our work output, our bodies consume this extra fat and then begin burning protein by breaking down our muscle tissue. If this undernourishment or starvation continues, we lose lean body mass, energy, and the ability to think clearly. Our metabolism slows down, our electrolyte levels are thrown off, and our interest in sexual and social interactions, as well as our resistance to injuries and infections, drops precipitously. As we continue to waste away, cannibalizing ourselves, we grow increasingly frail, lethargic, and confused. One by one our different bodily systems shut down, and, if we don't reverse the process by getting some food, we die.

Being alive, then, means having a radical and constant need for food and that is just as true for humans as for any other creature. As Monika Hellwig writes in *The Eucharist and the Hunger of the World,* "to be human is to be hungry. Not to be hungry is to be dead."[3] Humans are eaters, not just recreational eaters, but beings who must eat to live.

When we know this about ourselves—that we are eaters and that eating and drinking are not just entertainments or amusements but what we do to stay alive—we come to see ourselves as radically and chronically hungry. And when we recognize ourselves as creatures who cannot live without chewing, chomping, and swallowing a regular diet of organic material—something that celebrating a sacrament about eating and drinking holds up before our eyes—we are forced to acknowledge that we are constitutively needy, contingent, and dependent beings who do not live by our own resources.

In the United States and other wealthy nations, many of us have been able to forget our hunger. The abundance of food in our refrigerators and supermarkets has hidden our neediness from us. Our appetite for food and drink has been so thoroughly satisfied that we—the most voracious consumers on the planet—go through most of our days and lives unaware of our hunger or our identity as eaters. As Hellwig notes, "Our hunger is satisfied so quickly, so easily, so continuously that we can easily forget that hunger is there at all; it does not intrude itself."[4] As a result, we who are never hungry are "unlikely to have compassion or concern for those who are constantly hungry." And so we are losing our capacity to care about the hunger of those hundreds of millions whose daily struggle is to find enough food to stay alive. That, in Hellwig's words, "is a great deprivation of [our] humanity."[5]

The vast majority of humans, however, have never had the luxury of forgetting their hunger or neediness. As Clive Ponting points out in *A Green History of the World,* "until about the last two centuries in every part of the world nearly everyone lived on the edge of starvation. . . . About 95 percent of the people in the world were peasants; directly dependent on the land and living a life characterized by high infant mortality, low life expectancy, chronic undernourishment and with the ever present threat of famine."[6] Even today Bread for the World Institute reports that 840 million people (one-seventh of the planet) are undernourished and cannot find an adequate and secure supply of food. In the last half-century a lack of food or clean water has killed nearly 400 million people, three times the number that died in all the wars of the twentieth century.[7]

There is nothing good or noble about the hunger and malnourishment that have stalked humans for most of our history—and continue to stalk millions of the world's poor. Such a hunger stunts and brutalizes its victims. But there is some virtue in those of us who have forgotten our hunger coming to recognize our fundamental dependence on food. When we see ourselves as hungry eaters, and begin to imagine what it might be like to go without our daily bread (or cakes) for a few days or weeks, we begin to feel some sympathy and concern for the hundreds of millions of our neighbors who are haunted by a gnawing, crippling, and *eventually murderous* hunger. When we eat and drink consciously, knowing our own neediness, we are more likely to see and care about the hunger of those in soup lines and dining down at the local mission.

Eating and drinking as hungry people can also open our eyes to the hungers of many others who eat poorly or are tortured by disordered appetites. When we eat with an awareness of our own neediness, it is easier to feel sympathy and compassion for the hunger of today's "fasting girls," the millions of young middle-class women in this country who suffer from eating disorders. When we recognize our own hunger, we are more likely to feel solidarity with (and not superiority toward) these tortured young women. And when we see the power of our own appetites (and how they have driven the wealthiest fifth of the planet's population to consume 86% of all goods and services) it's easier for us to have compassion for millions of underclass American children who suffer from a life-threatening plague of obesity. Knowing ourselves as hungry eaters also helps to us to recognize, and perhaps even begin to feel, the desperate needs of the poor for other daily essentials like clothing, shelter, jobs, schools, and medical care.

When we know ourselves as eaters, then, we see the web of shared hunger that ties us to all the others begging for their daily bread. To eat and drink consciously is to find ourselves at table with the starving and malnourished, with the poor and oppressed, with the anorexic and obese. And to eat and drink consciously is to know our own hungers, including a deep and unaddressed hunger for God, creation, and our neighbor—and for justice and peace in our ties to these others. Seeing ourselves as hungry eaters and acknowledging our fundamental and permanent neediness helps us to recognize ourselves as the beggars and debtors we are, and to see that the only way we can come to the eucharistic banquet is as grateful and unworthy guests. The only possible response to this incredible act of graciousness on God's part is to share whatever we have been given with all the other beggars at the feast.

Food and Grace

But we are not just eaters. We are eaters who are being fed by others. Our food is grace. We do not create it; we receive it as a gift. It is God's gift, but—as we are reminded in the Eucharist—it is also the "fruit of the earth" and the "work of human hands," and other creatures provide and become this food for us. We eat from their bodies and sweat; from the fruit, leaves, seeds, and stalks of plants; and from the flesh of animals, borne to us by the labor of our neighbors.

We are eaters of the dead, and every meal we eat is the gift of some creature who has died or given a part of itself so we might be fed. In an essay on the Eucharist, Phillipe Rouillard puts this debt we owe those who become our food succinctly: "When I nourish myself, I am always eating a being which . . . has been killed for me, my life being preferred to its life. . . . In every act of nourishment there is a life sacrificed in order to permit another to have life and to have it abundantly."[8] Sallie McFague makes a similar point in *The Body of God*, reminding us that all forms of organic life need food from their environment, and that the more complex and so-called higher forms (like ourselves) are particularly dependent upon other creatures for our daily bread. Bacteria, plants, herbivores, and most carnivores (except some pets) could get along quite well without those of us perched at the top of the food chain, but we would find ourselves in very serious trouble should these other creatures start disappearing.[9] We should, Wendell Berry argues, always eat with gratitude, "for we are living from mystery, from creatures we did not make and powers we cannot comprehend." Citing the poet William Carlos Williams, Berry adds, "There is nothing to eat, seek it where you will, but the body of the Lord. The blessed plants and the sea, yield it to the imagination intact."[10]

Still, we do not just pick our daily bread off the stalk or vine, or pluck or butcher our daily portion of chicken or beef. This food arrives on our shelves and tables as "the work of human hands." Others have planted, watered, pruned, sprayed, picked, and packed, or canned it—or fed, raised, slaughtered, and sliced it. And often enough others have seasoned, cooked, prepared, and served our food, set our tables, washed our linens or dishes, and put out or collected our trash. Elves did not make our food. Farmers, ranchers, migrant workers, meat packers, truckers, grocers, butchers, checkers, and baggers, as well as cooks, waiters, and dishwashers brought our daily fare to the table. We eat from their sweat.

Recognizing our food as gift means at least three things. First, when we come to see the food and drink on our tables as grace, we acknowledge a threefold daily debt: (a) to God, who provides us with all our food and nourishment, (b) to all those fellow creatures who (directly or indirectly) have become food for us and/or sustain us through their being and activities, and (c) to all the people who labor to feed us—and indeed to all those whose labor down through the centuries has built up the agricultural processes and tools with which we are fed each day.

Second, if we eat from the flesh of other creatures and the sweat of other humans, we need to ask and care about what is being done to these plants and animals and neighbors who become and prepare our daily fare. What poisons or toxins were sprayed on fields or workers, injected into animals or plants? How were the chickens, pigs, or cattle, which ended up as our evening meal's main course raised, fed, or killed? Under what conditions do those who plant and harvest, butcher and package, or prepare and serve our meals labor? What are they paid? What risks do they run? What injuries do they suffer, and what (if any) compensations are they offered? Gratitude for our food means showing some concern for those whose flesh and sweat have been sacrificed to make this offering. We cannot, in good conscience, eat or give thanks for a meal laced with indifference, cruelty, or injustice.

Third, to see our food as gift means admitting that we too have a calling to be food for others. Eating and drinking consciously means knowing that our very life has been given to us as gifts, and that we are called to be gift to others. The food chain does not end with us. We are also expected to share our life with others. Genesis 2:15 tells us that humans were placed on the earth to take care of God's creation, to till it, and to look after it. We have a duty, then, to use our talents and labor to ensure ample food for the rest of creation and for the children and grandchildren who come after us.

Food and Pleasure

Cycling around New York's Finger Lakes under a bone-chilling drizzle, my friend Russ and I ducked into a small roadside diner where the chef's special was "Sweet Sue's Black Bean Soup." Watching us from her perch in the kitchen doorway, the amused and contented Sue savored the sight of two half-frozen and fully-sodden bikers reveling in each heaping spoonful of her dark spicy broth. I have rarely had so sweet a bowl of soup or known such pleasure under a slate grey sky.

We do not eat for calories alone, and a hot bowl of oatmeal laced with chunks of Granny Smith apple, chopped walnuts, and a dusting of cinnamon doesn't just fill our stomachs on a wintry morn, it gives comfort, warmth, and pleasure. We savor this hearty porridge's sweet scent, delight in its taste and texture as it rolls around in our mouths, relish the bouquet of flavors released from crushed fruit and nuts by our chomping teeth, and let out a sweet sigh of contentment as this simple breakfast of rolled oats warms our bellies and fortifies us for the day. As Browning wrote, "Morning's at seven . . . God's in his heaven, all's right with the world."

Astronauts may be satisfied with food that has no scent, flavor, or taste, which supplies us with the recommended daily dose of carbohydrates, minerals, and vitamins without providing a smidgeon of enjoyment. But the rest of us are more sensual creatures, and we enjoy the symphony of pleasures wafting our way from even the simplest fare. We love the fragrance of orange peels and the aroma of a roast chicken with a sprinkling of thyme. We delight in the taste of a patty of sweet butter melting on a slice of toast or dissolving in a baked potato lathered with sour cream and a scattering of bacon bits. And we revel in the warm pleasures of a glass of Burgundy, bearing to our palate the flavors of the soil, sunlight, and grapes.

Food pleases, delights, comforts, and nurtures us, and eating is one of the simplest, most powerful, and constant pleasures we know. We turn to food not just when we are hungry but when we are tired, cranky, weary, cold, and lonely—and we want our food not just to replenish our muscle tissues and blood cells but to lift our spirits and gladden our hearts. As Rouillard has written, when we are seated at table we wish to still our hunger, but we also seek "the pleasure of eating and eating well. For [us] a meal is not only a useful thing but a pleasurable thing."[11]

And this pleasure grows when it is shared. A late night slice of warmed-up apple pie is all the sweeter with a companion and a little conversation—particularly if she leaves a ridge of flaky crust on her finished plate. A bubbling tray of lasagna begs for a cluster of friends who will share the lip-smacking pleasures of this Parmesan-covered delight, and shower the cook and host with compliments and thanks. Though harried moms and dads might sometimes savor a solitary meal and envy the monk's peace and quiet, we tend to shy away from eating alone, especially in restaurants and on holidays. Potluck with friends is better than lobster for one. To enjoy food with others, to see the pleasure in their faces, and to feel the warmth and laughter in their hearts sweetens any meal we eat.

And that pleasure can be even sweeter when we break outside our regular circle of friends and family and make new companions by breaking bread with strangers, or by sharing food with those who are hungry. Many of us who as teens or young adults were cajoled or pressed to volunteer at a local soup kitchen or help serve a holiday meal to the homeless took up this task with a sense of fear and reluctance but discovered an unexpected pleasure in being of some use and offering hospitality to hungry women and men. The awkward burden became a privilege, and when we returned home to sit down with our own families and savor the Thanksgiving feast, our dining pleasure was all the sweeter for having been able to provide some cranberry sauce, oyster dressing, and a basted turkey breast or drumstick to folks who had been strangers to us.

Imagine, then, the pleasure if on some evening we knew that not only were our bellies and the bellies of all our friends and families warm and full, but that the parents and children in all the houses in our town and land and world had had a good meal. What a sweet pleasure that would be, to know that everyone from Budapest to Botswana to Bangladesh to Beijing had enjoyed the delights and comfort of a hearty meal, and that just once not a single child on the planet was going to wake up hungry. Jesus' disciples had some foretaste of this pleasure when they gathered in the twelve baskets of leftover loaves and fishes, and Jesus invites us to imagine such a sweet pleasure when he suggests that the reign of God will be like a banquet at which every beggar can sit down and eat their fill. When I was a child, our pastor told us that at every moment a Mass was being celebrated somewhere in the world. What a pleasure it would be to think that every time we celebrated the Eucharist we were breaking bread and sharing food with neighbors around the world, and that wherever this bread was being blessed, broken, and shared, there were baskets of leftovers.

The pleasure of eating is also enriched when we know our food: when the carrots, corn, and pork chops on our plates are not just packaged products of factory farms but produce and meat that came from a particular place, region, and farm—a place we know or at least know something about. It's not just our imagination that the watermelons, cherries, and tomatoes we buy at farmers' markets, roadside stands, or local co-ops taste so much sweeter than anonymous prepackaged food we pick up at the supermarket. We know this food better, can imagine it being picked off the stalk or vine, and are more certain about what has (and has not) been done to it.

Berry makes this point about pleasure and knowing our food in the following way:

> The pleasure of eating should be an *extensive* pleasure, not that of the mere gourmet. People who know the garden in which their vegetables have grown and know that the garden is healthy will remember the beauty of the growing plants, perhaps in the dewy first light of morning when gardens are at their best. Such a memory involves itself with the food and is one of the pleasures of eating. The knowledge of the good health of the garden relieves and frees and comforts the eater. The same goes for eating meat. The thought of the good pasture, and of the calf contentedly grazing, flavors the steak.[12]

When we know our food, Berry adds, we "eat with understanding and with gratitude. A significant part of the pleasure of eating is in one's accurate consciousness of the lives and the world from which food comes."[13]

Knowing ourselves as eaters, then, awakens us to the moral ties that bind us to others. When we come to see ourselves as hungry eaters and recognize our food and drink as a gift that is both the "fruit of the earth" and the "work of human hands" and let ourselves experience the full depth of the pleasure of eating, then our eyes are opened to all the others who are hungry with us, to those who ache to feel the pleasure of a good meal, to those who give their lives to become our food, and to those who toil to bring this food to our tables. When we eat consciously, we never dine alone.

America's Dis-Ease with Food

Several years ago the *New York Times* film critic Suzanne Hamlin suggested that Americans were ashamed of eating. Characters in foreign films, Hamlin noted, continue to do something that the stars of American movies have long since given up—they eat. Actually, they *dine,* and on more than a few occasions they pause to taste, savor, and relish the snacks, meals, and banquets being prepared and served with such gusto and, yes, love. *In Tampopo, Babette's Feast, Eat Drink Man Woman, Like Water for Chocolate, Antonia's Line, A Chef in Love,* and the more recent *Chocolat,* films from Japan, Denmark, Taiwan, Mexico, the Netherlands, Russia, and France, have given food a sensuous and starring role, celebrating meals as a sacrament of human (and divine) passions and of the ties that connect us to one another.

And yet, American movies "are woefully bereft of good food and great meals that bring people together in any kind of sensual, multifaceted way."[14] Indeed, even in those rare American films like Barry Levinson's *Avalon,* Stanley Tucci's *Big Night,* and Ang Lee's *Tortilla Soup,* where food is given a central role, these meals are portrayed as lost relics of our immigrant ethnicity, our foreignness. Once we become real Americans, our food disappears.[15] Complaining that our fascination with antiseptic kitchens, junk food, and fad diets has left us without a life-giving food culture, Hamlin commented that "What Americans don't seem to have is food important enough to even momentarily flash on the screen."[16]

Michelle Stacey speaks similarly about America's dis-ease with food in *Consumed: Why Americans Love, Hate, and Fear Food.*[17] Increasingly torn between a Jekyll obsession—with nutrition and dieting—and a Hyde addiction—to junk foods that are fast, fried or frosty, Stacey sees Americans as missing out on both the delicious pleasures of good food and the humanizing powers of great meals. American chef and anthropologist Mark Miller reports to Stacey that our Puritan background and clinical approach to nutrition have isolated us from the rich textures and "soft tissues" of food. "Food," Miller notes, "would make you sensual, it would make you real, it would make you alive."[18] But Americans, he argues, are so concerned with eating efficiently and living longer that we sacrifice a food culture that might make us alive. French chef Jaques Pepin adds that "the enjoyment of food (and the rituals that codify and often intensify that enjoyment) is knit into the very fabric of society, acting as a civilizer, a bond between peoples, a celebration of life itself." But in America, Pepin contends, "people have lost a great deal of that. They want to go into a corner and just swallow something in two seconds and think they're saving their life."[19]

Too Much Dieting

As Stacey argues, the first symptom of American dis-ease with food can be found in our national obsession with dieting, and in the millions of young women (and a growing number of men) who suffer from eating disorders. The increasing fascination with and magical beliefs about nutrition and weight loss have so skewed our relation to food and meals that *dieting,* no longer a mere fad, is becoming the "normal" way of eating for most Americans. According to Stacey "obsessing about food is more than a national pastime: it's on its way to becoming a national disorder." With some researchers arguing that "normal eating now requires periodic dieting," it increasingly sounds like we are living in "Diet America."[20]

In this "Diet America," self-control has become "the key to our new way of eating." Eating well here no longer means enjoying the pleasures and companionship of a good meal, but rather exercising some ascetical self-control that will allow us to live thin and disease-free. Food, which now has a moral—sometimes even magical—quality based on its fat content, nutritional value, or recently discovered medicinal properties, has been "transformed from a source of sustenance and pleasure to a test of resolve and a wellspring of power, moral superiority, and even class status."[21] In "Diet America" more and more of us are reportedly trying to control our eating so we can have flat abs, long life lines, and a certain moral advantage over the heavyset.

Life in this dieting nation is particularly tough on women. In a recent piece in the *New York Times* Jane Brody reports that

> some eight million people, mostly women and mostly young, suffer from anorexia, in which they starve themselves, or from bulimia, in which they gorge and purge. According to a survey by the Mayo Clinic, the incidence of eating disorders has risen by 36 percent every five years since the 1950s.[22]

Writing on religion and food, Margaret Miles adds that "over 90% of eating disorders occur in young middle class women," and that "a recent study at Harvard University showed that one in ten college women suffer from eating disorders."[23] Stacey reports that a recent clinical report has 80–85% of American women experiencing an eating disorder at some point in their lives.[24]

Too Much Fa(s)t Food

Ironically enough, the second symptom of our nation's dis-ease with food is a growing plague of obesity. As Eric Schlosser reports in *Fast Food Nation,* "Diet America" is becoming the land of food that is fast and fat, and citizens that are only one of the above:

> Over the last three decades, fast food has infiltrated every nook and cranny of American society. . . . Fast food is now served at restaurants and drive-throughs, at stadiums, airports, zoos, high schools, elementary schools, and universities, on cruise ships, trains, and airplanes, at K-Marts, Wal-Marts, gas stations, and even at hospital cafeterias. In 1970, Americans spent about $6 billion on fast food; in 2000, they spent more than $110 billion. Americans now spend more money on fast food than on higher education, personal computers, computer software, or new cars. They spend more on fast food than on movies, books, magazines, newspapers, videos, and recorded music—combined.[25]

And one result of all this fast and fattening food is a spreading epidemic of obesity.

> The United States now has the highest obesity rate of any industrialized nation in the world. More than half of all American adults and about one-quarter of all American children are now obese or overweight. Those proportions have soared during the last few decades, along with the consumption of fast food. The rate of obesity among American adults is twice as high today as it was in the early 1960s. The rate of obesity among American children is twice as high as it was in the late 1970s.[26]

Today about forty million American adults (20%) are obese, and more than 55% of us are overweight. Every year more than 280,000 people in the U.S. die as the result of being overweight, and obesity (which is now the country's second-leading cause of mortality) costs our nation's healthcare system nearly $240 billion.[27]

Unfortunately, much of the weight of all this extra fat falls on our minorities and underclass. Greg Critser argues in "Let Them Eat Fat," that obesity is a class issue in America, and study after study indicates that minorities and the poor are more likely to be obese than their white middle- and upper-class neighbors:[28]

> Federal statistics show that rates of obesity climb as poverty increases, particularly among minorities. While about 16 percent of whites who earn about $50,000 a year are obese, that rate climbs to nearly 23 percent among those whites who earn about $15,000. On the other hand, 22.5 percent of blacks who earn $50,000 are obese, but that figure rises to nearly 34 percent for those blacks who make about $15,000.[29]

Lack of access to supermarkets with ample produce sections or schools with adequate physical education programs—as well as greater reliance on television as the babysitter and recreation of choice and a growing dependence on fast food franchises that serve "super-size" meals—all contribute to higher rates of obesity among our nation's poor. Meanwhile, the diet of United States' upper class shows more and more signs of health and low-fat restraint. In the *New York Times*'s piece on "The Morality of Fat," Molly O'Neill is not surprised that the U.S.A.'s well-off are able to eat a healthier diet and remain slimmer. "It costs more to cook healthfully. It takes more time. It requires certain knowledge and certain expertise. . . . Statistically, affluent and well-educated shoppers are more likely to buy raw ingredients, while the less privileged are more likely to buy processed foods."[30]

Too Much Hunger

The third symptom of America's dis-ease with food is the lingering presence of hunger in the midst of plenty. According to the Bread for the World Institute website, even through the economic boom of the late '90s the number of hungry Americans remained stable:

> Thirty-one million people live in households that experience hunger or the risk of hunger. This represents one in ten house-

holds in the U.S. . . . . The U.S. Conference of Mayors reported
that in 1999, requests for emergency food assistance in 26 major
cities increased for the fifteenth year in a row—by an average of
18 percent.[31]

In 1997 America's Second Harvest, the country's largest network
of food banks, reported that 21 million people came seeking food
from their agencies, and that 40% were from working families. In
Nickel and Dimed, Barbara Ehrenreich notes that in 1999 food pantries
in Massachusetts, Texas, and Georgia were nearly swamped by increasing demands, that food banks across the country were facing "a
torrent of demand which (they) cannot meet," and that in Wisconsin
the percentage of food stamp families in "extreme poverty" was up
to 30%.[32]

Unconscious Eating in America

Much of our dis-ease with food in America flows from the fact
that we have become unconscious eaters, for the American way of
eating in this century has cut most of us off from the "religious" or relational meaning of food, and we do not know what we are doing
when we eat. We are ignorant of our dependence on or connection to
others, and we certainly have little sense of participating in mystery.
Our modern means of food production and delivery have so alienated U.S. consumers from the agricultural, economic, and political
processes of eating that our food might as well be made by elves. And
though we are proud of the variety and abundance with which our
supermarket shelves are regularly stocked, we have little or no idea
where the "products" we drop into our carts come from; who planted,
grew, and picked them; or what has been done to them along the way
to this store.[33] As Jack Nelson wrote in *Hunger for Justice* over twenty
years ago, "millions of our children grow up believing that the origin
of food is the supermarket. They, and many of us as well, no longer
appreciate the delicate interface between creation, soil, and human
labor."[34] In all our rush to transform food into an efficiently manu-
factured, packaged, and delivered product we have lost its "soft, con-
nective tissue." It ties us to nothing and no one, and we do not feel its
blessing.

Eating the "Fruit of the Earth" Unconsciously

We eat "the fruit of the earth" unconsciously when we do not know or care what has been done to the soil and plants that bore the grains and produce what we consume—or what sort of diet and steroids fattened up the livestock being grilled in our backyard barbecues. We eat unconsciously: when we do not pause to ask about the millions of square miles of tropical rain forests being destroyed to provide grazing land for cattle; when we do not ask what is being done to our rivers, lakes, and aquifers to supply irrigation for America's agribusinesses; when we do not wonder about the environmental impact of huge monoculture plantations raising mile after mile of genetically-engineered and pesticide-coated fruits and vegetables. We eat unconsciously when we don't ask about the suffering of cattle, pigs, and chickens raised in factory farms, or about the ecological harm of pumping millions of tons of animal waste into the local water system. We eat unconsciously when we don't pause to ask what our consumption of meat is doing to the planet.

Since the invention of agriculture we humans have eaten in a way that has stressed our local environments. Indeed, humans have generally exploited our environments to the best of our ability (or technology) and have often exhausted these places and been forced to move on to greener pastures.[35] Numerous societies from the Mediterranean to Central America to China and to the Indus valley have degraded and exhausted their local environments in an attempt to sustain a growing human population and increasingly complex civilizations. Along with many others, the Sumerian, Greek, Roman, Arabian, and Mayan civilizations deforested lands, degraded and destroyed habitats, drove or hunted species into extinction, and eroded and exhausted soil by the processes of human agriculture and expansion. As the environmentalist Peter Farb noted, "from the very beginning *Homo [sapiens]* has exploited the environment up to his technological limits to do so," the result often being the desertification and collapse of regional ecosystems in Mesopotamia, North Africa, central Mexico, northern China, and the Indus valley.[36] Ancient farmers eventually transformed Babylon's Fertile Crescent into a desert, and the Roman Empire's North African breadbasket is now part of the Sahara.

Until fairly recently the harmful effects of our ways of eating have been rather limited, but with European colonialism, and then the industrialization of agriculture, the impact of our diet on the rest of creation has grown ever more burdensome. In Asia, Africa, and the Americas lush forests and environments rich with a cornucopia of flora and fauna were cut or burned down and replaced with huge plantations producing single (and usually foreign) crops for export back to Europe. Today "half the forests that once covered the earth are gone, . . . [and] each year at least another 16 million hectares (about 40 million acres) of natural forest are razed—an area the size of Washington state."[37] The Philippines has lost 92% of its rain forest. Brazil has lost 95% of its Atlantic coastal forest. Old growth forests in West Africa, India, Madagascar, and elsewhere are a tenth of their original size. "By the middle of the next century . . . tropical forest will exist virtually nowhere outside of protected areas—that is, national parks, wildlife refuges, and other official reserves."[38]

The destruction of native ecosystems by modern agriculture has led to the extinction of countless plants and animals, as have our ever more-expanded and efficient methods of hunting and fishing. Currently we are in the midst of what may be the most massive extinction of species in 65 million years. Conservative estimates indicate that we could lose one-third of all species on the planet before this process is done. Others suggest numbers as high as two-thirds.[39] At present nearly half of the 233 nonhuman species of primates are facing extinction, while about a quarter of the vertebrate species are considered to be in serious trouble. About "25 percent of mammals and amphibian species, 11 percent of birds, 20 percent of reptiles, and 34 percent of fish species surveyed so far are threatened with extinction."[40]

The growth of industrialized agriculture and factory farms in the twentieth century has had other harmful effects as well. The increasing reliance on single-crop plantations has led to astronomical increases in the use of pesticides and herbicides. In the quarter-century after 1953 "the amount spread on crops in the developed world rose fifteen fold."[41] Our growing reliance on irrigation has placed tremendous pressures on our water supply, significantly increased the salinity of our rivers and crop lands, and escalated our loss of topsoil. Farmers worldwide now lose about 24 billion tons of topsoil from their crop land every year. The Colorado River often runs dry before it reaches the sea, as do the Ganges in India and the Jordan in the Middle East. In 1997 the Yellow River failed to reach its mouth on 226 days. And the U.S.'s Ogallala Aquifer, one of the world's largest groundwater reserves, has already been half-depleted from irrigation. Meanwhile, in the U.S., animal waste from raising nearly 200 million livestock pollutes our water with over two billion tons of wet manure a year, more than ten times the amount of solid waste generated by all our municipalities combined.[42]

The animals being raised in our factory farms also pay a high price for the privilege of being part of our daily bread. In the drive to produce more and cheaper meat for our dinner tables and fast food restaurants, we have transformed the family farm into a mechanized agribusiness, and our fellow creatures have been reduced to products without any rights or claims on our respect or concern. Cattle, pigs, chickens, and other animals are raised in extremely small cages, sties, or stalls—often chained in place, denied access to light or movement, and fed an artificial diet rich in growth hormones and antibiotics. As Ponting notes,

> During the twentieth century animal rearing systems have become more intensive. Instead of feeding outdoors on natural foods such as grass, animals have been brought indoors into highly artificial environments and fed on artificial feeds. Chickens are kept in overcrowded battery cages, cattle in small stalls and pigs are chained to walls in sties small enough to ensure that they cannot move. Animals, which are herbivores, are fed on a diet which may include a high percentage of dead animals, recycled manure, growth hormones and also antibiotics to control the diseases that would otherwise be rife in such conditions.[43]

Schlosser gives an equally depressing description of the conditions in massive feedlots where cattle are prepared for slaughter:

> Each of [these feedlots] can hold up to one hundred thousand head of cattle. At times the animals are crowded so closely together it looks like a sea of cattle, a mooing, moving mass of brown and white fur that goes on for acres. . . . A government health official . . . compared the sanitary conditions in a modern feedlot to those in a crowded European city during the Middle Ages, when people dumped their chamber pots out the window, raw sewage ran in the streets, and epidemics raged. The cattle now packed into feedlots get little exercise and live amid pools of manure.[44]

These are painful things to hear, but if we are going to eat the "fruit of the earth" with any real awareness, then we need to know our food and to know what is being done in our name to the bounty of God's creation and to the creatures that become our daily bread. As politicians are often fond of reminding us, "there is no free lunch," and we need to know the full cost of the meal we sit down to eat.

Eating the "Work of Human Hands" Unconsciously

We eat food that is the "work of human hands" unconsciously when we do not know or attend to those whose labor has brought this food to our tables. We eat this bread unconsciously when we do not care about the planter, picker, packer, trucker, or server who bears and fashions our food, when we are unaware or unconcerned about their low wages or poor working conditions. This food bears the sweat of many others, and not to know or care about what they suffer in the process of preparing our daily bread is to be an unconscious but genuine collaborator in injustice.

Before the development of agriculture, about ten thousand years ago, humans lived in small tribes of hunter-gatherers who moved about in search of fresh supplies of food. Collecting and preparing food was a daily concern in these tribes, and this work was shared in a fairly egalitarian fashion. With the invention of agriculture, however, human societies were able (with significantly more work) to stay in one place and produce enough food so that a minority of people could be freed up to specialize in other tasks. Some became artisans. Others were scribes, clerics, soldiers, builders, metalworkers, and rulers. Villages grew up and became cities and then empires. But in these increasingly stratified and hierarchical agricultural societies the small elite class of nonfarmers still needed their daily bread and depended on a vast sea of slaves, serfs, and peasants to provide it for them. So the princes and high priests sent out their tax collectors and soldiers, took enough to fill their granaries and barns with all the foodstuff and livestock they wanted, and then retreated to their banquet halls to dine off the sweat of those who worked in the fields. In the centuries and millennia that followed, this practice was repeated by Caesars, colonial powers, and plantation owners.

With the coming of the industrial revolution and the mechanization of farming, modern societies no longer needed 90% of their population working in agriculture. "In the middle of the nineteenth century, for example, a *majority* of the population was engaged in agriculture. By 1900 that had dropped to one-third, by 1940 one-fifth, and today to just under three percent. . . . By 1990 no developed country had more than five percent of the workforce in farming."[45]

Still, though they now represent a small minority of the workforce, we do need to be concerned about those who labor to prepare our daily bread. In this country we have made a commitment to keeping the consumer's food bill low, with the result that "Americans today spend less of their disposable income on food than any people in any other industrialized country."[46] But with food prices at an historic low we need to ask ourselves if we are paying a just wage for our dinner.

Between 1935 and 1983 4,500,000 U.S. farms disappeared or were swallowed by agribusinesses. Since 1979 the number of family farms in this country has fallen by 300,000, and multinational agribusiness corporations have gained more and more control over farm production, commodities, and markets. According to the U.S. Catholic bishops, this "loss of farms and the exodus of farmers from the land has led to the loss of a valued way of life, the decline of rural communities, and the increased concentration of land ownership."[47] Schlosser agrees, noting that

> farmers and cattle ranchers are losing their independence, essentially becoming hired hands for the agribusiness giants or being forced off the land. Family farms are now being replaced by gigantic corporate farms with absentee owners. Rural communities are losing their middle class and becoming socially stratified, divided between a small wealthy elite and large numbers of the working poor.[48]

And the plight of farm workers is noticeably worse. According to the U.S. Catholic Conference/Office of Migration and Refugee Services, agriculture is a dangerous and difficult occupation:

> Seasonal agricultural laborers are exposed to dangerous pesticides; suffer repetitive motion injuries; have limited access to housing and sanitation; do not have meaningful opportunities to organize or collectively bargain to improve their situation; and earn poverty or sub-poverty level wages without receiving bene-

fits. In 1999 the average yearly income of an adult farm worker was less than $7,500.[49]

In the U.S. migrant farmworkers (and their children) are exposed to a wide range of health risks from pesticides—including a fourfold increase in the risk of skin disease, increased risks of developing several different kinds of cancer, and an increased occurrence of sterility, birth defects, brain damage, and Parkinson's.[50] Meanwhile, a recent study indicates that as many as 25 million agricultural workers in the developing world are poisoned by pesticides each year.[51]

But our farmers and farmworkers are not the only ones making sacrifices to bring us our daily bread. Schlosser argues that life is no picnic for workers in the meatpacking or food service industries either:

> Meatpacking is now the most dangerous job in the U.S. The injury rate in a slaughterhouse is about three times higher than the rate in a typical American factory. Every year about one out of three meatpacking workers in this country—roughly forty-three thousand men and women—suffer an injury or a work-related illness that requires medical attention beyond first aid.[52]

And as for the folks behind the counter, serving up our burgers and fries:

> The restaurant industry is now America's largest private employer, and it pays some of the lowest wages. During the economic boom of the 1990s, when many American workers enjoyed their first pay raises in a generation, the real value of wages in the restaurant industry continued to fall. The roughly 3.5 million fast food workers are by far the largest group of minimum wage earners in the United States. The only Americans who consistently earn a lower hourly wage are migrant farm workers.[53]

In *Waiting: The True Confessions of a Waitress,* Debra Ginsberg chronicles two decades as a waitress and makes it clear that although Americans spend nearly a billion dollars a day dining out, we have little regard or esteem for the two million people who bring us our menus, meals, and desserts. According to Ginsberg, waiters and waitresses are held in such low esteem that most people who wait on tables full time prefer not to tell others what they do for a living, and male contestants on a recent game show identified "waitressing" as the occupation they would least like their wife to have.[54]

The Eucharist presents a striking challenge to this unconscious eating of the "work of human hands" and this ingratitude and disrespect toward those who prepare and bring our food to us. In the Gospel of John's account of the Last Supper, Jesus himself takes up the apron of a server and comes around to wash the feet of his dinner guests. And in the differing versions of the multiplication of the loaves story Jesus gives his disciples the task of distributing the bread and fish to the seated crowd, which may explain why in the early Church the twelve apostles had the job of handing out the daily portions of bread to all the members of the community, and why later this honored role was given to seven Christians considered to be full of faith and the Holy Spirit (Acts 6:2-6).

Unconscious Consumers

Still, it's not just our unconscious consumption of food and drink that is problematic. Americans have also become the most unconscious consumers of all things great and small on the planet. Seventy percent of us visit the mall each week, more than go to church or synagogue. We spend six hours per week shopping and only about forty minutes playing with our children, which may explain why we have more malls (about 40,000) than high schools in the U.S., or why, in spite of the fact that our houses are twice as large as they were in the 1950s, we currently need twenty-five times as many commercial self-storage units to put our stuff in as we had in 1970. This may even explain why more than a quarter of the households making more than $100,000 per year claim they can't afford everything they "need."[55]

In his 1845 classic *Democracy in America,* Alexis de Tocqueville gives us an early insight into our American appetite for consumption, noting in us what he considered "an inordinate love of material gratification."[56] Nor was he alone in this opinion. Alexander Hamilton commented on the tendency his fellow citizens had for "multiplying their acquisitions and enjoyments," a penchant that has not disappeared in the intervening two centuries. Since the 1950s Americans have used more resources than everyone who ever lived before them. With less than 5% of the world's population we consume about 60% of the world's natural gas, 40% of its coal, and 30% of its petroleum.

Indeed, one estimate indicates that if every other nation copied our patterns of consumption it would take the resources of four earths to keep up.[57]

Fueling our appetite for consumption is a huge advertising industry. The average American sees one million commercials before registering to vote, and another million before collecting Social Security. At present, Madison Avenue spends a bit more than $500 per year on every man, woman, and child in this country, and we spend about a year of our life watching commercials. Marketers are particularly interested in preaching the gospel of consumption to our youngsters, and they have increased spending on children's advertising by tenfold in the last fifteen years, hoping to "brand" them early and produce loyal, lifelong customers. The underlying message of this media barrage is simple: Happiness may be achieved through ownership and/or consumption of the latest product. Indeed, such ownership or consumption is necessary to achieve or maintain the grace, beauty, power, popularity, and/or status we all supposedly seek.[58]

Tragically, this conspicuous consumption is going on side by side with desperate poverty at home and abroad. While the U.S. consumes one quarter of the world's energy, and millions of Americans spend disposable income on Lexuses, Rolexes, and sports utility vehicles costing up to $40,000, one-seventh of the planet is hungry or chronically malnourished. Our overconsumption of resources and our preference for private consumer goods over public spending on basic needs is an injustice against the poor. And our present patterns of consumption pose severe ecological threats. For along with consuming one quarter of the planet's energy, the U.S. accounts for 25% of global carbon dioxide emissions and overall pollution, and the U.S. leads the world in per capita production of garbage. Each of us generates about 1,300 pounds of trash and uses up to 20 tons of raw materials per year, recycling only the tiniest fraction of these resources.

As we will see below, the Eucharist has a great deal to say about our duties to share and to refrain from hoarding.

The Eucharist and Eating Consciously

"Do this in remembrance of me" (1 Cor 11:24). In the Eucharist we remember and celebrate the death and resurrection of Jesus, and when we eat this bread and drink this cup we partake in this redemptive mystery. We also remember and celebrate our hunger and God's grace, and this sacrament of eating and drinking demands that we eat and drink mindfully, gratefully, and generously.

As already noted, when we eat and drink of this bread and wine we invoke not just the memory of the Last Supper.[59] We also remember and celebrate Jesus feeding the hungry multitudes, for here too he takes bread, blesses and breaks it, and distributes it to his disciples.[60] We remember as well God providing food for the Hebrews wandering in the desert, and we remember the promise of a heavenly banquet to which a host of hungry beggars and outcasts will be invited and welcomed. Whenever we celebrate the Eucharist attentively and seek to eat and drink this bread and wine worthily we are pressed to remember our own hunger and neediness, as well as the desperate hunger of all the poor and sinned against. And we are reminded of the lavish generosity of the God who feeds us each day, and of our vocation to share food and hospitality with the poor and hungry, indeed to be food for others.

Remembering Our Hunger and the Hunger of the Poor

"Before we can begin to understand . . . the Eucharist," Monika Hellwig argues, "or try to fathom the message it conveys, we need to remember hunger." For "the simple, central action of the Eucharist is the sharing of food—not only eating but sharing. [And] the simple, central human experience for the understanding of this action is hunger."[61] We eat to satisfy our hunger, and we share food in response to the hunger of our sisters and brothers. To celebrate this sacrament about eating and sharing food, then, we must remember our own hunger and the hunger of our poor neighbor.

Unfortunately, as Hellwig notes, many of us have forgotten our hunger, and go long stretches without remembering the hunger pangs of neighbors who struggle for scraps to supply their daily bread. So we come to the Eucharist unprepared to feast or to share our food and lives with those who have nothing but their naked hunger. Regis Duffy argues that we who have forgotten our hunger suffer from a false sense of abundance and a "sinful satiety."[62] We do not remember our desperate need for God and do (or will) not see the terrible need of our neighbor. Like the rich man in Luke's parable about the beggar

Lazarus (16:19-31), our property and goods give us a false sense of abundance and deafen us to the hungry cries of our own hearts or of the poor man who sits at our gate.

This "sinful satiety" keeps us from feasting at the Eucharist because it prevents us from seeing our desperate need for God's generosity. Time and time again in the Gospels it is only the beggars and paupers who find a place at the heavenly banquet. For "only the needy will set up a lusty cry for God's gift. . . . [T]he Kingdom of God can offer little to one who believes that he has all."[63] "Blessed," then, as Luke 6:21-25 tells us, "are you who are hungry now, for you will be filled. . . . [But] [w]oe to you who are full now, for you will be hungry." For the hungry know that they need God, and their hunger has made a space in them to celebrate God's bounty.

This "sinful satiety" also anaesthetizes us to the hunger of our neighbors, and thus impedes our celebration of a sacrament of eating and *sharing*. Paul chastises the wealthy Christians in Corinth for the unworthy fashion in which they eat the Lord's Supper (1 Cor 11:17-34). Indeed, the disciple tells these well-to-do believers that they are not eating the Lord's Supper at their gatherings, for they gorge themselves while the poor in their company go hungry. To eat in this way, to ignore the hunger of their fellow Christians, is a violation of the tradition of the Eucharist that Paul has handed onto them. Such assemblies, Paul assures the Corinthian community, do more harm than good, and they are not being done in memory of the one who came to be food for others.

Finally, this false abundance makes it even more difficult for us to authentically celebrate the Eucharist when such a "sinful satiety" has been secured, as it often is, by taking or hoarding the very bread which belongs to the hungry poor. As Enrique Dussel notes, when the poor are hungry because they have not been paid a fair wage for the "work of human hands" that brings food to our tables, then we eat a bread leavened with injustice and offer an idolatrous sacrifice in place of the Eucharist.[64] We cannot eat the bread or drink the cup of the Lord worthily if we anesthetize our own hunger by putting hunger in the mouths of the poor.

In the Eucharist we celebrate a meal that anticipates the banquet of God's kingdom, and all who come to this table must come as beggars to a feast. And in this same memorial meal we sit down with all sorts of other hungry women and men; with Jacob and his children gone down to Egypt in hopes of escaping a famine, with the Hebrews wandering in the wilderness, with the multitudes come out to a lonely place to see Jesus, and with those poor Christians in Corinth who did not have enough to eat. Indeed, at this beggar's banquet we sit down with all the widowed, orphans, and aliens who ever needed the generosity and hospitality of strangers, with all the men and women who ever stood in a soup line, with the vast majority of the human race that has, down through the ages, lived on the edge of starvation, and with the more than 800 million of our neighbors who continue to do so today. And we sit down with the one who has never forgotten the hunger of the poor, who has made that hunger his own, who tells us in Matthew 25:35, "for I was hungry and you gave me food, I was thirsty and you gave me something to drink."

Eating and sharing food in the Eucharist means hearing the cries of hunger rising from all these neighbors, and recognizing in ourselves the deep hungers and appetites that are not fed but masked and anesthetized by our riches and accomplishments. As Hellwig argues, in any authentic celebration of the Eucharist "the needs of the poorest and the most oppressed are constantly being voiced among us to challenge us and reveal the state of sin and selfishness in which we live."[65] At this table we see ourselves and our neighbors as hungry beggars, and the Eucharist reminds us that our own deepest hunger for God's feast will be satisfied to the degree that we remember and respond to the hungers of our neighbors. Give us our daily bread *as* we share bread with those who hunger with us.

Remembering God's Graciousness

Still, it is not just—or even primarily—our hunger that we remember in the Eucharist. It is God's bounty and generosity. In the Eucharist we are remembering with gratitude that God is the source of all our bread, of all our food and drink, of all our lives. The word "Eucharist" comes from the Greek *eucharisteō*, which means to give thanks, and when Jesus "blesses" *(eucharisteō)* the bread and wine at the Last Supper (and the loaves and fish in the multiplication narratives) he is giving thanks to the one who has brought forth the fruit of the earth and the work of human hands. So in the Eucharist we bless and thank God for our food and lives and for our salvation in Christ. For as Hellwig notes, a grace over meals is not in the first place a blessing of food but a blessing of God who is the source of this food and of all life and sustenance. . . . [And] to bless God is to acknowledge him as the source of blessings, to honor him with praise and thanksgiving.[66]

In the Eucharist, then, we remember God as the source of all our food and sustenance. We remember God providing food for all creation in Genesis 1:29-30:

See, I have given you every plant yielding seed that is upon the face of all the earth, and every tree with seed in its fruit; you shall have them for food. And to every beast of the earth, and to every bird of the air, and to everything that creeps on the earth, everything that has the breath of life, I have given every green plant for food.

And we remember God telling the children of Noah (Gen 9:3) that "Every moving thing that lives shall be food for you; and just as I gave you the green plants, I give you everything." So too we remember the psalmist (Ps 104:24-28) praising God, proclaiming that "the earth is full of your creatures. . . . [and] [t]hese all look to you to give them their food in due season; when you give to them, they gather it up; when you open your hand, they are filled with good things."

We remember too in the Eucharist the bread that God rained down upon the Hebrews during their long sojourn in the wilderness, the manna which Moses told his people was "the bread that the LORD has given you to eat" (Exod 16:15). And we remember God miraculously sustaining the prophet Elijah and a widow and her son for years on a single handful of wheat and a little oil (1 Kgs 17:7-16), and multiplying loaves of barley set before Elisha to feed a crowd of a hundred men (2 Kgs 4:42-44).

And, of course, the bread that is blessed, broken, and distributed in the Eucharist evokes the memory of Jesus' miraculous feeding of the multitudes, an event that is recorded six times in the Gospels (Mark 6:14-29, 8:1-10; Matt 14:13-21, 15:32-39; Luke 9:10-17; and John 6:1-13). And we remember Jesus' promise in John 6:35 that "I am the bread of life. Whoever comes to me will never be hungry, and whoever believes in me will never be thirsty."

The Eucharist also has us remembering and anticipating the heavenly or messianic banquet, that great and lavish feast that announces the reign of God and to which our prodigally generous Lord invites a host of beggars, paupers, and outcasts. Isaiah 25:6 tells us that "On this mountain the LORD of hosts will make for all peoples a feast of rich food, a feast of well-aged wines, of rich food filled with marrow, of well-aged wines strained clear." And in the New Testament Jesus repeatedly uses the image of a sumptuous feast as the symbol of God's reign.

Finally, in the Eucharist we remember that while all our food and nourishment is a gift from God, this same sustenance is also the fruit of the earth and the work of human hands, so our giving thanks *(eucharisteō)* to God embraces as well all those creatures and persons who have become and borne this meal to us. As Phillipe Rouillard notes,

> every morsel of bread is the product and the result of an entire history. First, in the season for planting the grains of wheat are thrown into the bosom of the earth, which is a fertile mother, and after an apparent death and time of gestation and germination, man, marveling, sees a blade grow.[67]

And this wheat, which the earth has borne forth, becomes food on our table only after a number of humans have labored to water, harvest, grind, mix, bake, package, and deliver it to us. "This bread, which has required the work of so many hands and the know-how of so many people, . . . is much more than an element of nourishment: it is a symbol of work," and of the generosity of the creatures and persons who have borne it to us.[68] Eating and drinking this eucharistic bread and wine, then, calls us to remember, bless, and give thanks to those who have become and prepared this meal—and all our meals.

From Memory to Mission

If the Eucharist calls us to remember our own hunger and the hunger of the poor and sinned against, as well as the bounty of God and the generosity of our fellow creatures and neighbors, what does this remembering oblige us to do or become? If being a eucharistic people means being a community of mindful eaters, how should this mindfulness show itself? If Hellwig is right that the central act of the Eucharist is the eating and *sharing* of food, then a eucharistic community must always be a community that, like Jesus, shares food with the hungry and works to dismantle every unjust structure that deprives or robs the poor of their daily bread.

For when we eat and drink bread and wine in the Eucharist we remember Sarah and Abraham welcoming hungry strangers with a lavishly sumptuous meal (Genesis 18), and we recall Abraham's nephew Lot doing the same when these hungry visitors arrive in Sodom (Genesis 19). We remember as well the generosity of Boaz (Ruth 2), offering food and a meal to the impoverished widow and alien, Ruth, and we call to mind the compassion of the widow of Sidon sharing her last scraps of food with the prophet Elijah (1 Kgs 17:7-16). In the breaking of the bread we are reminded of the abundant mercy of the prodigal's parents (Luke 15:11-32), celebrating a sinner's homecoming with an embarrassment of riches, and we recoil at the rich man's murderous indifference (Luke 16:19-30), failing to offer even table scraps to the beggar Lazarus.

And in this sacrament of eating and sharing food we are reminded of the wondrous sharing of bread that took place among the Hebrews in the wilderness. As Joseph Grassi notes, the miracle of God's feeding the Israelites with manna was accompanied by a second miracle of sharing food:

> In the story every able-bodied person went out to gather the miraculous bread. Some were able to gather large amounts, others very little. Yet God commanded that at the end of the day all should share equally, regardless of the amount they had gathered. In this way all the people, the sick, the old, the handicapped, had enough.[69]

As Exodus 16:18 tells us, "those who gathered much had nothing over, and those who gathered little had no shortage."

And God's command to share food with the hungry does not end with the Hebrew's sojourn in the desert. In Leviticus 19:9-10 the Lord tells the Israelites that "When you reap the harvest of your land, you shall not reap to the very edges of your field, or gather the gleanings of your harvest. You shall not strip your vineyard bare, or gather the fallen grapes of your vineyard; you shall leave them for the poor and the alien." And in Leviticus 25 God demands that every fifty years any poor Hebrews made homeless or driven into servitude must be given back their lands, so they will have access to crops and food. Being a faithful Hebrew means remembering the hungry.

Jesus repeats this command to feed the hungry to his own disciples in the Gospel accounts of the multiplication of loaves and fish. For when the disciples urge Jesus to "send the crowds away so that they may go into the villages and buy food for themselves," he responds that "They need not go away; you give them something to eat" (Matt 14:15-16). And in spite of their fears about having too little to feed this huge crowd, the disciples follow Jesus' instruction to share their meager portion of blessed and broken loaves with the multitude and discover that God has multiplied their shared offering a thousand fold.

And in Luke 14:12-14 Jesus tells us that "When you give a luncheon or a dinner, do not invite your friends . . . or rich neighbors. . . . [I]nvite the poor, the crippled, the lame, and the blind." These impoverished and hungry guests have no way of repaying us, but God will bless and remember the food we have shared with the poor, for as Jesus says to those who have fed the hungry, "Truly I tell you, just as you did it to one of the least of these who are members of my family, you did it to me" (Matt 25:40).

In the early Christian community the followers of Jesus, who had come to recognize and remember Christ in the breaking of the bread, understood that feeding the hungry was a critical part of being a disciple and taking part in the Eucharist. The church in Jerusalem "gave their testimony to the resurrection of the Lord Jesus" (Acts 4:33), and did this by breaking bread together and by sharing all their goods and property, so that none of them were needy (Acts 2:44-45; 4:32-35). And until the community there grew too numerous it was the responsibility of the twelve apostles to distribute the daily portions of food to the community, and to ensure that the widows and orphans received a fair share. When this became too difficult, the community appointed a special ministry of seven holy and spirit-filled disciples to ensure that food was distributed to the poor, and the first of these, Stephen, became the early Church's first martyr.

As already noted, when Paul hears that the community in Corinth is attempting to celebrate the Eucharist *without* sharing food with the hungry (1 Cor 11:27), he chastises them: "Whoever, therefore, eats the bread or drinks the cup of the Lord in an unworthy manner will be answerable for the body and blood of the Lord," and later Paul encourages the same community to imitate the example of generosity to the poor offered by the church in Macedonia (2 Cor 8:1-15). From this and other passages it seems clear that throughout the New Testament "discipleship is closely connected to sharing food with the hungry."[70] Indeed, as the Catholic bishops of Canada have noted, "Whatever else may be said about the social thrust of the Scriptures, the fraternal responsibility to feed brothers and sisters who are hungry is a central imperative."[71]

William Crockett argues that the close link found in the New Testament between the Eucharist and care of the hungry shows up as well in early Christian liturgies and writings:

> There was a close relationship in the early liturgies between the offering of gifts and the care of the needy. In his account of the liturgy in Rome in the middle of the second century, Justin Martyr tells us that those who have the resources "come to the aid of all who are in need, and we are always assisting one another." During the Sunday liturgy, the contributions of the wealthy are deposited with the one who presides, and "he helps orphans and widows, and those who through sickness or any other cause are in need, and those in prison, and strangers sojourning among us; in a word, he takes care of all those who are in need."[72]

Even today, Crockett contends "the community that gathers to celebrate the Eucharist cannot . . . share the eucharistic bread and cup without reflecting on what that means for Christian obedience in a world of economic disparity, where many go hungry every day."[73] There is a link between what we are doing when we eat and share the bread blessed and broken in the Eucharist and what we are doing when we do or do not come to the aid of our hungry neighbors. Our participation in the Eucharist makes demands upon us, not just to share some of our personal wealth with the hungry, but to confront and reform any and all economic and political practices and structures that make it difficult or impossible for the poor to secure their daily bread. We cannot eat and drink the Lord's Supper worthily in a world where over 800 million go to bed hungry and where so many millions of those who prepare our food are underpaid unless we live out our eucharistic identity by remembering and addressing the hunger and poverty of our neighbors.

Unfortunately, we Christians have not always paid very close attention to the social implications of eating and drinking at the Eucharist. Down through the ages we have often spiritualized and domesticated the Eucharist, ignoring or forgetting our duties to other hungry eaters, and to those who become and prepare our food. Monika Hellwig comments that "after centuries of Christianity, with the message of sharing and simplicity of life, preached and enacted in the Eucharist, one would expect that in Christian nations the difference between rich and poor would no longer be so great and that the poor would at least not be destitute."[74]

As we know, that is not the case.

Still, the Eucharist itself offers us reason for hope. For although we, like the disciples in the Gospel accounts of the multiplication of the loaves and fishes, are frightened by the challenge of feeding so many with such meager portions, the Eucharist celebrates our faith in a God who multiplies bread that is shared. This God empowers us to overcome the divisions and tear down the structures that keep the poor from securing their daily bread. The God we remember and proclaim in the Eucharist enables us to share our lives and food in a way that provides enough food and basic goods for all.

Notes

[1] The commands, as they appear in the different eucharistic prayers, are based on Matthew 26:26-27.

[2] See, among others, Joseph A. Grassi, *Broken Bread and Broken Bodies: The Lord's Supper and World Hunger* (Maryknoll, N.Y.: Orbis, 1985); Monika Hellwig, *The Eucharist and the Hunger of the World,* rev. ed. (Kansas City, Mo.: Sheed & Ward, 1992); William R. Crockett, *Eucharist: Symbol of Transformation,* (New York: Pueblo, 1989); Enrique Dussel, "The Bread of the Eucharistic Celebration as a Sign of Justice in the Community," in *Can We Always Celebrate the Eucharist?* ed. Mary Collins and David Power, Concilium 152 (New York: Seabury Press, 1982) 56–65; R. Kevin Seasoltz, "Justice and the Eucharist," *Worship* 58 (1984) 507–25.

[3] Hellwig, *Eucharist,* 3.

[4] Ibid.

[5] Ibid.

[6] Clive Ponting, *A Green History of the World: The Environment and the Collapse of Great Civilizations* (New York: Penguin Books, 1991) 88.

[7] Bread for the World Institute, "Hunger Basics: Frequently Asked Questions," www.bread.org/hungerbasics/faq.html.

[8] Phillipe Rouillard, "From Human Meal to Christian Eucharist," *Worship* 52 (1978) 427.

[9] Sallie McFague, *The Body of God: An Ecological Theology* (Minneapolis: Fortress, 1993) 57–59; 106–7.

[10] Wendell Berry, "The Pleasures of Eating," in *Not for Bread Alone: Writers on Food, Wine, and the Art of Eating,* ed. Daniel Halpern (Hopewell, N.J.: Ecco, 1993) 17.

[11] Rouillard, "Meal to Eucharist," 431.

[12] Berry, "Pleasures of Eating," 17.

[13] Ibid.

[14] Suzanne Hamlin, "*Le Grand Excès* Spices Love Poems to Food," *New York Times,* 31 July 1994, sec. H.

[15] Levinson's 1990 film *Avalon* makes this point quite starkly, using the shift from a large family banquet to individual TV trays as a metaphor for the Americanization of a Russian-Jewish family.

[16] Hamlin, "Le Grand Excès," sec. H.

[17] Michelle Stacey, *Consumed: Why Americans Love, Hate, and Fear Food* (New York: Simon & Schuster, 1994). Also of interest is Harvey Levenstein's *Paradox of Plenty: A Social History of Eating in Modern America* (New York: Oxford University Press, 1993).

[18] Stacey, *Consumed,* 199.

[19] Ibid., 10, 207.

[20] Ibid., 178–79. See also Annetta Miller, "Diets Incorporated," *Newsweek,* 11 September 1989, 56–60.

[21] Stacey, *Consumed,* 172. Molly O'Neill makes a number of the same points in "The Morality of Fat," *The New York Times Magazine,* 10 March 1996, 37–39.

[22] Jane E. Brody, "Exposing the Perils of Eating Disorders," *New York Times,* 12 December 2000, sec. F.

[23] Margaret R. Miles, "Religion and Food: The Case of Eating Disorders," *Journal of the American Academy of Religion* 63 (1995) 552.

[24] Stacey, *Consumed,* 178.

[25] Eric Schlosser, *Fast Food Nation: The Dark Side of the All-American Meal* (Boston: Houghton Mifflin, 2001) 3.

[26] Ibid., 240.

[27] Ibid., 241–42; Lindsay Tanner, "Nearly 20% of Adults in U.S. Obese, Study Says," *Seattle Times,* 13 September 2001, sec. A, 4th edition.

[28] Greg Critser, "Let Them Eat Fat: The Heavy Truths About American Obesity," *Harper's,* March 2000, 41–47.

[29] David Barboza, "Rampant Obesity, A Debilitating Reality for the Urban Poor," *New York Times,* 26 December 2000, sec. F.

[30] O'Neill, "The Morality of Fat," 39.

[31] Bread for the World, "Domestic Hunger and Poverty Facts," www.bread.org/hungerbasics/domestic.html.

[32] Barbara Ehrenreich, *Nickel and Dimed: On (Not) Getting By in America* (New York: Metropolitan Books, 2001) 218–19.

[33] Jack Hilt, "The Theory of Supermarkets," *The New York Times Magazine,* 10 March 1996, 56–61, 94, 98.

[34] Jack Nelson, *Hunger for Justice: The Politics of Food and Faith* (Maryknoll, N.Y.: Orbis, 1980) 155.

[35] Larry L. Rasmussen, *Earth Community, Earth Ethics* (Maryknoll, N.Y.: Orbis, 1997) 38–43.

[36] Peter Farb, *Ecology* (New York: Time-Life, 1970) 164.

[37] Janet Abramowitz, "Worldwatch Press Release on Forests," 4 April 1998, 1.

[38] David Quammen, "Planet of Weeds," *Harper's,* October 1998, 62.

[39] Ibid., 61, 65.

[40] John Tuxill, "Worldwatch Press Release on Vertebrate Declines," 23 May 1998, 1–2.

[41] Ponting, *A Green History,* 247.

[42] Michael Brower and Warren Leon, *The Consumer Guide to Effective Environmental Choices: Practical Advice from the Union of Concerned Scientists* (New York: Three Rivers Press, 1999) 59.

[43] Ponting, *A Green History,* 247–48.

[44] Schlosser, *Fast Food Nation,* 150, 201–2.

[45] Rasmussen, *Earth Community,* 65.

[46] U.S. Catholic Bishops, *Economic Justice for All* in *Catholic Social Thought: The Documentary Heritage,* eds. David O'Brien and Thomas Shannon (Maryknoll, N.Y.: Orbis, 1992) 628.

[47] Ibid.

[48] Schlosser, *Fast Food Nation,* 8.

[49] U.S. Catholic Bishops Office of Migration and Refugee Services, "H-2A Agricultural Workers," http://www.usccb.org/mrs/h2a.htm.

[50] Marion Moses, "Farmworkers and Pesticides," in *Confronting Environmental Racism: Vices from the Gassroots,* ed. Robert Bullard (Boston: South End, 1993) 162–69.

[51] Sachs, *Eco-Justice,* 39–39.

[52] Schlosser, *Fast Food Nation,* 172.

[53] Ibid., 6.

[54] Debra Ginsberg, *Waiting: The True Confessions of a Waitress* (New York: HarperCollins, 2000) 112, 130.

[55] Andrew Hacker, *Money: Who Has How Much and Why* (New York: Scribner, 1997) 38–43; Juliet B. Schor, *The Overspent American: Upscaling, Downshifting, and the New Consumer* (New York: Basic Books, 1998) 3–24, 67–109.

[56] Alexis de Tocqueville, *Democracy in America,* trans. George Lawrence, ed. J. P. Mayer (New York: Doubleday, 1969) 506.

[57] Allen R. Myerson, "U.S. Splurging on Energy after Falling Off Its Diet," *New York Times,* 22 October 1998, sec. A; J. Milburn Thompson, *Justice and Peace: A Christian Primer* (Maryknoll, N.Y.: Orbis, 1997) 63–81.

[58] Neil Postman, *Amusing Ourselves to Death* (New York: Viking, 1986) 104–5, 126–37; Benjamin Barber, *Jihad vs. McWorld* (New York: Ballantine, 1996) 59–62.

[59] Rouillard, "From Human Meal to Christian Eucharist," part 2, *Worship* 53 (1979) 45; Seasoltz, "Justice and the Eucharist," 519.

[60] Rouillard, "Meal to Eucharist," part 2, 45; Joseph A. Grassi, *Loaves and Fishes: The Gospel Feeding Narratives* (Collegeville: The Liturgical Press, 1991) 45–46, 56, 69.

[61] Hellwig, *Eucharist,* 2–3.

[62] Regis Duffy, "Symbols of Abundance, Symbols of Need," in *Liturgy and Justice,* ed. Mark Searle (Collegeville: The Liturgical Press, 1980) 72–90.

[63] Ibid., 74.

[64] Dussel, "The Bread of the Eucharistic Celebration," 56–65.

[65] Hellwig, *Eucharist,* 80.

[66] Ibid., 40–41.

[67] Rouillard, "Meal to Eucharist," 428.

[68] Ibid.

[69] Grassi, *Broken Bread and Broken Bodies,* 51–52.

[70] Ibid., 56.

[71] Canadian Catholic Bishops, "Sharing Daily Bread," Labor Day Message, 2 September 1974 (Ottawa: Canadian Catholic Conference, 1974) 2–4.

[72] Crockett, *Symbol of Transformation,* 255.

[73] Ibid., 251.

[74] Hellwig, *Eucharist,* 49.

Chapter Two

The Breaking of the Bread

A School for Manners

Like many large families, ours had a number of rules, and a lot of them were about eating. We were not to eat between meals, take food or drink into the living room or bedrooms, start eating before everybody else was served (and especially no "digging in" before guests!), talk with food in our mouths, make weird faces or noises while eating, interrupt other people while they were speaking, or leave the table before asking to be excused. We were expected to wash our hands and faces before dinner, help out with setting the table, washing the dishes, or taking out the trash, sit up straight at the table, wait for grace to be said before eating, say "please" and "thank you" occasionally, and eat all our vegetables before asking for dessert.

Growing up, I tended to think of these rules as an annoyance. But in the college cafeteria I ran across people who had been raised without eating rules, and the dining experience was noticeably less pleasant. Standing in line behind a guy who took the last five desserts, looking for any spot where the previous diners had cleaned up behind themselves, or sitting across from a roommate who was chewing and chatting simultaneously made me homesick in a whole new way. I wanted to move in with *The Waltons*, the family show of television fame.

I soon figured out that all those rules weren't just about eating—they were about meals. Our parents were teaching us how to eat *together,* how to eat with other people, and by extension, how to work and play

39

and live with other people. Our meals and meal rules were a school for manners, a daily practice teaching us how to get along with and show respect for one another. More than etiquette and politeness, we were learning how to share, how to wait our turn, how to pitch in and help out, how to pay attention and listen, how to treat one another with regard, how to show gratitude and courtesy, and how to make guests feel welcome. At these meals we were doing more than filling our bellies. We were celebrating and practicing being a family and being schooled in hospitality, friendship, and service.

The Eucharist is also a meal. More than just eating and drinking, the Eucharist is about breaking bread with others, about sharing food and drink, about sitting down at table with one another. In the Eucharist we are made "companions" (from the Latin for "sharing bread with") of Christ and of all the other beggars, strangers, and outcasts who have been offered hospitality, friendship, and service at his table.

The author of Luke and Acts uses the phrase "the breaking of the bread" to describe the Eucharist, and tells us that the early disciples not only recognized and remembered the risen Christ in this breaking of the bread, but also shared their lives with one another in and through these common meals. And these disciples sought to practice the hospitality, friendship, and service Jesus had taught them in his own table fellowship.[1] In the Eucharist we celebrate and remember the Last Supper and all the Gospel meals in which Jesus broke bread with both friends and strangers, and we take part in a feast that anticipates the heavenly banquet at which we will all sit down at God's table and break bread with one another. At the same time, this Eucharist connects and reconciles us with one another, and in the Eucharist we celebrate and practice being a *koinonia* (community) and *ekklesia* (church) that is formed in the image and likeness of Christ, and schooled in his table manners.

For the Eucharist, too, is a school for manners, a school where we celebrate and learn how to be Christians, how to be Church. In the New Testament Jesus does a good deal of his teaching at meals. This instruction consists not just of the advice or reprimands he directs at hosts and fellow guests, or the parables he tells about the heavenly banquet, but also (even primarily) of the ways in which he conducts himself at these meals. Time after time the Gospel authors portray Jesus as someone whose table manners are at odds with those around him, as a teacher who practices a radical style of table fellowship, whose notions of hospitality, friendship, and service offer a revolutionary challenge to the world around him and to those who would be his disciples.[2] When we celebrate the Eucharist we are not just being fed by God's manna, we are being schooled in Jesus' manners, and they challenge us to practice an ethic of hospitality, friendship, and service that imitates Christ, anticipates the heavenly banquet, and transforms the world we live in.

In order to grasp the radical nature of the table fellowship we find Jesus practicing in the New Testament, we need to know something about the table manners and meal practices he is challenging, and we need to understand what these practices and rules were teaching people about hospitality, friendship, and service. Two sets of table manners that would have been on the minds of the Gospel authors who wrote about Jesus' table manners were associated with the symposium and the Passover.

In the ancient Greco-Roman world of Jesus' day, the symposium was a formal banquet and a model of the perfect or ideal meal at which host and guests shared not only a fine dinner but also a rich evening of conversation and conviviality. Throughout the Mediterranean these stylized dinner parties were a common way for political, social, and religious groups of all sorts to gather and celebrate common bonds and discuss important matters, and they had an established structure and etiquette that defined how hosts and guests and servants were to conduct themselves and treat one another.[3]

Guests were invited to a symposium, and upon arriving for what was normally an evening meal, the host's servants brought them to the dining area and helped them to take their place, reclining on one of the couches arranged around a central table. The servants then washed the guests' feet. The servants brought the guests bowls in which to wash their hands and served their meal. Only free men were allowed to recline at these meals (women and slaves had to sit), and guests took their place around the room according to their rank or status, with the most important guest being seated to the right of the host. After the meal had been eaten, guests and host were served wine and either entertained with dancing and music or treated to a serious conversation on a topic of importance.

The symposium served as a school for manners in two different ways: Since these banquets were held up as a model of human conviviality and peacefulness, their rules of etiquette were seen as an ideal description of how people should treat companions, strangers, and persons of differing station and class, indeed, how they should practice hospitality, friendship, and service. And because the second half of these dinner parties was often given over to serious conversations about philosophical and ethical questions, an ancient writer like Plato would use the symposium as a literary form to teach the thought of Socrates by offering the philosopher's insights in the form of an after-dinner dialogue.

The writers of the Gospels also use stories about meals to teach their readers a way of life, and the tales of Jesus breaking bread and parables about the messianic banquet are meant as a school for manners for anyone who would be a disciple of Christ. In the New Testament most of the meals that Jesus attends and banquets he describes have a structure quite like the symposium. There are invitations, guests, hosts, and servants washing feet and preparing food, as well as conversations about honored places around the banquet table. And a good deal of Jesus' teaching takes place in the context of one of these meals. But, as we will see, Jesus' practice of table fellowship and his notions of hospitality, friendship, and service turn the world of the symposium on its head.[4] Hospitality is to be shown not to esteemed and noble guests but to needy beggars, bringing the poor, the blind, and the lame in off the street. Friendship extends not only to one's dinner companions, but also to women and slaves, sinners and outcasts, strangers and enemies. And masters are not to recline and have their feet washed by unseen servants, but to get up from their couches and take up the servant's basin and towel.

The Gospel accounts of the meals of Jesus, and in particular of the Last Supper, are also set against the backdrop of the Passover and all the sacred meals celebrating the covenant between God and the Hebrews. In the Passover meal Israel remembers and celebrates her identity as God's chosen, her liberation from Egypt, and in this celebration Israel also looks forward to the coming of the Messiah. The authors of the New Testament see Jesus as the fulfillment of these hopes for liberation and redemption—and his Last Supper and passion and death as the new Passover. What is distinctive, however, about this meal, and about the table fellowship that Jesus practices, is that this new banquet is open to *all* the people of the world.[5] Gentiles, Samaritans, and every other race, tribe, and nationality are welcome. Again and again in the Gospels, Jesus practices and preaches a table fellowship that stretches beyond the boundaries of family and nation, a table fellowship that invites guests from the north, south, east, and west to sit at the heavenly banquet.

In this chapter, then, we will explore the Eucharist as a radical school for manners, the Eucharist as a meal in which we celebrate and practice being disciples and companions of Christ. And, like the early disciples who recognized and remembered Christ in "the breaking of the bread," we will try to figure out what it means to be Christians by contemplating and imitating the table fellowship of Jesus. In particular, we will examine his practice of hospitality to those in need, friendship to outcasts and sinners, and service to the lowly.

Hospitality: Making Room for the Poor

An Ancient Virtue

Today we see hospitality as a form of courtesy shown to dinner guests, and we consider our church a place of hospitality if parishioners make new members feel welcome. But as Christine Pohl notes in *Making Room: Recovering Hospitality as a Christian Tradition,* for centuries Christians saw hospitality as a basic moral virtue required of every disciple and community. More than courtesy among friends, hospitality demanded offering food, shelter, and protection to needy strangers.[6] Indeed, it called for breaking bread with those in need, welcoming them as guests and companions.

"Most of the ancient world," Pohl reports "regarded hospitality as a fundamental moral practice. It was necessary to human well-being and essential to the protection of vulnerable strangers."[7] In a world without hotels or credit cards, strangers and sojourners depended on the hospitality of the communities they entered to secure food, shelter, and any sort of a welcome. Homer reminds us repeatedly in *The Odyssey* that the gods showered their blessings on those who showed hospitality to travelers like Odysseus, and the gods cursed those who did not.

The Old Testament contains a number of stories about God blessing hospitality—and punishing its absence. Abraham and Sarah welcome three strangers approaching their tent in the noonday heat, offering their guests a shady place to rest, water to wash off the dust of the road and a sumptuous meal (Genesis 18). As a reward God blesses Sarah (who was barren) with a child. When two of these strangers travel on to Sodom (Genesis 19), Abraham's nephew Lot also offers them hospitality, but the men of Sodom attempt to violate Lot's guests, and God destroys the city for its incredible inhospitality.

In 1 and 2 Kings we find two stories of God blessing foreign women for their hospitality to wandering prophets. Sent by God to the town of Zarephath, Elijah receives hospitality from a poor widow on the brink of starvation. God blesses this generosity by sustaining the widow, her son, and their guest throughout a long drought (1 Kings 17–18). The prophet Elisha receives unexpected hospitality from a wealthy Shunammite woman who has her husband build a spare room for the traveling holy man. Like Sarah, she is blessed with a child (2 Kgs 4:8-37).

Israel had its own reasons for showing hospitality to strangers. The Scriptures reminded the Hebrews that they too had been aliens and sojourners, that only God's hospitality had liberated them and brought them safely through the wilderness, and that they were now obliged to show this same hospitality to any stranger or sojourner in their midst.

"When an alien resides with you in your land, you shall not oppress the alien," God tells the Israelites in Leviticus, "The alien who resides with you shall be to you as the citizen among you; you shall love the alien as yourself, for you were aliens in the land of Egypt" (19:33-34). Those who fail to show this hospitality have failed to honor the God who "who executes justice for the orphan and the widow, and who loves the strangers, providing them food and clothing" (Deut 10:18). As YHWH tells the Hebrews in Isaiah 58:6-7, the one fast required of them is "to loose the bonds of injustice, to undo the thongs of the yoke, to let the oppressed go free, and to break every yoke? Is it not to share your bread with the hungry, and bring the homeless poor into your house; when you see the naked, to cover them, and not to hide yourself from your own kin?"

Each year, then, they were to leave a portion of their fields to be harvested by the sojourner and the landless poor (Lev 19:10), and every fifty years those who were driven off their land by poverty were to be welcomed back to their homesteads (Lev 25:25-28). In a land where everyone was an alien and all were guests of God, hospitality was to be denied to no one.

Jesus and Hospitality

In the New Testament Jesus is both the stranger in need of hospitality and the generous host proclaiming and practicing the hospitality of God's heavenly banquet. The infant for whom there was no room in the inn, the child driven into exile, and the itinerant preacher without a place to rest his head is also the one who breaks and shares bread with hungry crowds that have followed him out into the wilderness. In a series of meals taken with friends and strangers Jesus preaches and practices a hospitality that makes room for the poor and the needy and that calls his disciples to do likewise.

The most familiar example of Jesus as a gracious host is the story of the multiplication of the loaves and fishes. Each of the four Gospels has an account of this meal (Matt 14:13-21; Mark 6:30-44; Luke 9:10-17; John 6:1-21) and two of them have versions of what may be a second such miracle (Matt 15:32-39; Mark 8:1-10).

In *Dining in the Kingdom of God,* Eugene LaVerdiere describes the miracle of the loaves and fishes as a "hospitality meal." A large crowd of people has followed Jesus out to a lonely and deserted place, and as evening draws on most of these men, women, and children are growing tired, hungry, and cold. They will soon need food, drink, and lodging, but are a long walk from any town where they might find such provisions, and Jesus' disciples are overwhelmed by the prospect of providing for such a huge crowd. In many ways the five thousand tired and hungry sojourners are like the tribes of Israel traveling through the wilderness. It will take a miracle to provide for all of them, in this lonely place, the miracle of God's hospitality.

When the disciples ask Jesus to dismiss the crowd and send these thousands of tired and hungry people into the nearby towns and countryside in search of food and lodging he will not do so. The one who has been moved with compassion at the sight of these needy sojourners will not turn them away to find hospitality elsewhere. Nor will he let his disciples retreat from their duty to show hospitality to these guests. "There is no need for them to go," he says to the twelve, "you give them something to eat" (Matt 14:16). And so he has the disciples bring him the only food they can find, invites the five thousand to sit down for an evening meal, takes the five loaves and two fish, looks up to heaven, and blesses, breaks, and shares this meal with his five thousand guests.

In this "hospitality meal" Jesus teaches his disciples to practice the table fellowship of God's heavenly banquet, to make room for the poor, and to welcome the needy at one's table. And when we take, bless, break, and share bread in the Eucharist we remember this example of hospitality and we recall the commands to "give them something to eat" and to "do this in memory of me." For hospitality to the needy is to be a hallmark of the disciple of Christ.

In Luke 14, Jesus is a dinner guest in the home of a leading Pharisee and in his table talk Jesus advises his host not to imitate the world's hospitality, which is extended only to those who might return or reward it. "When you give a luncheon or a dinner, do not invite your friends or your brothers or your relatives or rich neighbors, . . . But when you give a banquet, invite the poor, the crippled, the lame, and the blind" (vv. 12-13). And later, in a parable about the heavenly banquet, Jesus notes that God will be making a special place for those needy strangers who are left off the guest list of most dinners (vv. 15-22).

Jesus drives home this command to show hospitality to the needy in two of the best known Lukan parables, the Good Samaritan (10:29-37) and the story of the rich man and the beggar Lazarus (16:19-31). In each of these parables hospitality to those in need is the basic requirement for anyone hoping to be invited to sit down at the heavenly banquet.

Responding to a lawyer who asks, "[W]hat must I do to inherit eternal life?" (Luke 10:25), Jesus tells the story of a traveler who has been brutally assaulted and left for dead. Both a priest and a Levite pass by the desperately wounded sojourner without offering any help. But a Samaritan (to whom our wounded traveler would almost certainly *not* have offered hospitality) is moved with compassion and stops to care for this needy stranger. Washing and bandaging his wounds with lavish care, and paying for food and lodging until the injured man recovers, the Samaritan is a walking definition of the hospitality Jesus demands of his disciples. This, Jesus tells the lawyer, is what is required to dine in the kingdom of God, "Go and do as he did."

The second parable, however, recounts the tale of a wealthy man who breaks bread every day within sight of a poor starving beggar without offering the sore-covered Lazarus so much as a scrap from his lavish table. When the beggar dies he is taken up into the bosom of Abraham and receives the hospitality of God's heavenly banquet. But the rich man's passing brings him to exile in Hades, where he tastes the miseries he had ignored in Lazarus. And when he begs for even the smallest sign of hospitality—a mere drip of water on his parched tongue—the rich man learns that his own inhospitality has condemned him to stand outside the banquet hall forever.

The parable of the last judgment (Matthew 25) also underscores the importance of hospitality to the poor and reminds us that Jesus is both the needy stranger who begs for our hospitality and the host of the heavenly banquet. As we have treated one, so will the other treat us. Welcoming the righteous into the heavenly banquet, the Son of Man tells them, "Come, you that are blessed by my Father, inherit the kingdom prepared for you from the foundation of the world; for I was hungry and you gave me food, I was thirsty and you gave me something to drink, I was a stranger and you welcomed me. . . ." (vv. 34-35). The righteous reply, "Lord, when was it that we saw you hungry and gave you food, or thirsty and gave you something to drink? And when was it that we saw you a stranger and welcomed you, or naked and gave you clothing? And when was it that we saw you sick or in prison and visited you?" The righteous are asking, When Lord, did we show you such hospitality?—the sum of all the questions—the Lord replies, "Truly I tell you, just as you did it to one of the least of these who are members of my family, you did it to me" (v. 40).

In word and deed Jesus practices and proclaims a table fellowship that embraces and demands hospitality to those in need. In the miracle of the loaves and fish; in his table talk with others; and in his parables about the heavenly banquet, the Good Samaritan, the rich man and the beggar Lazarus, and the last judgment, Jesus preaches a radical hospitality to those in need, and he commands the same of anyone hoping to sit down at the messianic banquet.

This command to show hospitality is almost always presented in the setting of a shared meal. The miracle of loaves and fish is a "hospitality meal" at which Jesus sits down and breaks bread with his guests. His table talk about hospitality to needy strangers and the parable about God's banquet are offered in the setting of a Sabbath meal (Luke 14:1-24), and the rich man shows his grievous inhospitality by failing to share even the scraps of his table with Lazarus (Luke 16:19-31).

Shared meals are important because the hospitality Jesus is practicing and proclaiming involves more than just feeding the hungry and offering shelter and protection to the homeless. Imitating God's hospitality means sitting down at table with the poor and needy, breaking bread with them as our companions, and welcoming them into our homes and communities as our guests. In Luke 14, Jesus does not advise his host to go out and give food to the poor, the crippled, the lame, and the blind. He tells him to invite them as guests to his next lunch, dinner, or party.

We should, then, hear this call to hospitality every time we come to the Eucharist. For the Eucharist is the Christian community's shared meal *par excellence,* and here we celebrate, remember, and are called to practice the table fellowship of Jesus. This "breaking of the bread" is a memorial meal that connects us not just with the Last Supper, but with all the Gospel meals in which Jesus practiced and proclaimed hospitality. It is also the shared meal in which we celebrate and antici-pate the heavenly banquet and God's radical hospitality.

Eucharistic Hospitality

The author of Luke tells us that the early disciples recognized and remembered the risen Christ in "the breaking of the bread" (24:28-35), Luke's term for the Eucharist. And in Acts 2:42 the same writer re-ports that the first Christians devoted themselves to "the breaking of the bread," following Jesus' command at the Last Supper to "do this in memory of me" (Luke 22:19, *NAB,* 1975 Sacramentary).[8] But this Eucharistic community also responded to the call to "give them some-thing to eat." The same disciples who gathered regularly for "the breaking of the bread" likewise agreed to hold "all things in common; they would sell their possessions and goods and distribute the pro-ceeds to all, as any had need" (Acts 2:44b-45). According to Acts 4:34-35, "There was not a needy person among them, for as many as owned lands or houses sold them and brought the proceeds of what was sold. They laid it at the apostles' feet, and it was distributed to each as any had need."

Indeed, hospitality to the poor was so important in the early Church that the apostles themselves were entrusted with the daily distribution of food to the widows and others in need. Just as Jesus had commanded them to seat and serve the hungry multitude, so now they had the task of showing hospitality to the hungry and needy in their own midst. And when the community grew too large for the apostles to continue in this role, seven members "full of the Spirit and of wisdom" were selected and ordained for this critical task (Acts 6:1-6).

Other New Testament voices also testify to the importance of hospitality to the needy in the early Church. In Romans 12:13 Paul instructs his audience to "Contribute to the needs of the saints; extend hospitality to strangers." The author of 1 Peter tells his Christian readers to "Be hospitable to one another without complaining (4:9)." And in 1 Timothy 3:2, 5:9-10 and Titus 1:8 hospitality is listed as a requirement for leadership and ministry in the Church. As Pohl notes, the early Christian Church came to be identified with hospitality to the poor. "Hospitality to needy strangers distinguished the early Church from its surrounding environment. Noted as exceptional by Christians and non-Christians alike, offering care to strangers became one of the distinguishing marks of the . . . Church."[9]

And the call to practice hospitality to the poor was often connected with the Eucharist. Indeed, Christians seemed particularly aware of their duty to practice Jesus' hospitality at their own gatherings and assemblies. In 1 Corinthians 11:17-34 Paul chastises a group of well-off Christians for their behavior at the celebration of the Lord's Supper (Paul's term for the Eucharist). Some of them are in such a rush to eat that they leave a number of the poor in their company hungry and embarrassed. When they behave in this way, Paul writes, they are not celebrating the Eucharist nor honoring the Body of Christ. Meanwhile, the author of James 2:1-4 warns Christians against showing less welcome to the poor who come into their assemblies than they would offer to the rich. Such inhospitality dishonors God, who has chosen the poor to be heirs of the kingdom.

In the centuries that followed, Christians continued to stress hospitality to the poor, as well as the link between this practice and the Eucharist. In the fourth century Lactantius repeats Jesus' advise in Luke 14, writing that "the house of a just man ought not to be open to the illustrious, but to the lowly and abject."[10] Jerome tells the clergy of his day to "let poor [people] and strangers be acquainted with your modest table, and with them Christ shall be your guest."[11] As we noted earlier, Justin Martyr reports that at the Sunday Eucharist a collection for the poor is entrusted to the bishop, who then "helps orphans and widows, and those who through sickness or any other cause are in need, and those in prison, and strangers sojourning among us; in a word, he takes care of all those who are in need."[12] And in the *Didascalia apostolorum* (*The Teachings of the Apostles*, a third century text) bishops are instructed to show hospitality to any poor person who enters the Eucharistic assembly. "If a poor man or woman should arrive . . . and there is no place for them, then you, the bishop, with all your heart provide a place for them, even if you have to sit on the ground."[13]

During the twentieth century a number of Christian voices have recovered the connection between the Eucharist and hospitality to the poor. Virgil Michel, a Benedictine monk and liturgist, called for reforms in the liturgy that would awaken Christians to their vibrant communion with one another and to their duty to care for all those who make up the Body of Christ, particularly the poor and down-trodden.[14] Rev. Paul Furfey, a radical priest and professor of sociology, found in the Eucharist a social message that demanded social and economic reforms that would make room for the poor and the underclass in America.[15] And Peter Maurin and Dorothy Day preached and practiced a gospel of hospitality to the poor at *The Catholic Worker,* and found the inspiration and daily bread for their direct service and prophetic writing in the Eucharist and hospitality of Jesus.[16]

Present Challenges

Two thousand years after Jesus began proclaiming and practicing the table fellowship of God's heavenly banquet, too many of the poor remain outside our gates and are unwelcome in our homes and communities—and churches. In spite of a host of New Testament and Christian witnesses testifying to Jesus' command to show hospitality to those in need, much of the work of welcoming the stranger remains undone. Indeed, there are signs that the poor are increasingly less welcome in our midst.

At home and abroad the divide between rich and poor has grown steadily over the past several decades and is expected to continue to increase. In 1960 the richest fifth of the planet earned 30 times as much as the poorest fifth. In 2001 they made 74 times as much. Between 1996 and 2000 the two hundred richest people on the planet saw their wealth double. They now own more than the poorest one billion.[17] Meanwhile, the United States continues to have the greatest gap between rich and poor of any industrialized nation.

Here in the United States this financial gulf has been accompanied by a growing geographic divide, a chasm over which the poor find it ever harder to cross. More and more of our poor are excluded from the public spaces in our society and forced to live in separate, unequal, and decidedly unsafe places—outside the gates and gated communities of middle and upper class America. The public space of our downtowns, parks, and public squares has increasingly been replaced by malls and other private and commercialized properties where the poor and the car-less are unwelcome.[18] Suburban sprawl and the flight to gated communities has segregated our society into increasingly distant, disparate, and often hostile communities. Between 1970 and 1990 the number of people squeezed into ghettos, barrios, and slums nearly doubled, climbing to 8.5 million. These are crowded, unsafe, and blighted places without enough jobs, hospitals, clean air, or water—and without much access to their suburban neighbors.[19] Meanwhile, the largest prison building campaign in human history has put two million mostly poor, black, and uneducated Americans behind bars.[20] In the United States we make room for the poor, but only in lockup.

Our inhospitality has an ecological dimension as well. As noted in chapter 1, on eating, we humans have long overstressed and exhausted the environments we were supposed to be sharing with other beings. And in the age of colonialism and industrialization the impact of our appetites has exploded exponentially as we have encroached on and degraded the habitats of countless species, plowing down forests and overwhelming entire ecosystems. Instead of making room for all God's creatures great and small, our consumption and destruction of resources strips millions of creatures of their food and shelter and generating the most massive extinction of species since the disappearance of the dinosaurs.[21] Not only is there no room in the inn, there is now no room in the manger.

Sadly, even our eucharistic celebrations often fail to show hospitality to the stranger. Most of us belong to fairly homogenous parishes and churches where we have little real contact with people of different classes, races, or ethnic communities. As Kenneth Himes notes, "Large cathedral parishes in our downtown areas and urban service or shrine churches are some of the few truly heterogeneous gatherings in our society."[22] Outside of these rare exceptions Christians tend to break bread within socioeconomic monocultures, homogenized enclaves where nearly everyone is of the same color and tax bracket.

In the New Testament Jesus proclaims and practices a radical table fellowship that challenges those who would break bread with him to show hospitality to those in need. This hospitality to the poor became a mark of the early Church and was held up as a requirement for persons or communities that would call themselves Christian. Today the table fellowship of Jesus and the hospitality of the heavenly banquet continue to challenge us, demanding that in our homes, communities, churches, and planet we make room for the ones who stand at the gate. "I was a stranger" Jesus tells us, "and you welcomed me" (Matt 25:35).

Friendship: Welcoming the Outcasts and Sinners

The Eucharist is, as stated ealier, a meal. And though a TV dinner eaten in solitude while watching the evening news can be called a meal, we usually mean food and drink shared with others. As Phillipe Rouillard notes, "for a meal one is seated at table to nourish oneself but also to seek the company of others, to share with them, to nourish friendship and community."[23] At our common meals we celebrate and strengthen the social bonds that tie us to family and friends, we make new friends and welcome strangers into our midst as companions.

In the ancient world the common meal or Greco-Roman banquet also brought people together and celebrated the ties that bound them to one another.[24] Throughout the Mediterranean, groups of every sort and class used the banquet or symposium as a way to come together socially. This was true of families and friends gathering for a wedding feast, guild members having a memorial dinner for one of their dead, philosophical societies meeting for a heady conversation, or religious groups assembling for worship.

Those who broke bread together at these common meals were considered friends and felt a special obligation to one another. In his *Table Talk,* Plutarch mentions "the friend-making character of the table," and writes that, "a guest comes to share not only meat, wine, and dessert, but conversation, fun, and the amiability that leads to friendship."[25] This friendship created certain moral bonds, and ancient authors laid out a table ethic to be practiced toward dinner companions. Plato offered a set of banquet rules aimed at preserving this friendship, while other authors condemned rude or abusive conduct at table and warned against "factions" or divisive behavior.[26] Still, there were limits to this table friendship. Women, children, and slaves were generally excluded, as were other sorts of outcasts. The table friendship of Jesus would prove more extensive.

In John's account of the Last Supper (15:12-15), Jesus calls the disciples who break bread with him his "friends" and tells them this friendship means they are to love one another as he has loved them. Celebrating the Eucharist makes us friends of Jesus as well and generates a similar duty to love others *as Jesus has loved us*. Celebrating the Eucharist as friends of Jesus, then, means practicing a love that forgives sinners, welcomes outcasts, and befriends enemies.

Jesus teaches us this love or friendship at table. In his table fellowship and parables about the heavenly banquet Jesus proclaims and practices a friendship that forgives sinners and invites them to repent and forgive one another. This same table fellowship is a sign of reconciliation challenging us to make peace with all the other friends of Christ. At the table of the Lord, sinner and outcasts are welcomed and the wounds dividing Jew and Greek, slave and free, male and female are finally healed.

The Friend of Sinners and Outcasts

We first learn of Jesus breaking bread with sinners in the story of Levi (or Matthew), a tax collector who has left everything to follow Jesus (Mark 2:13-17, Matt 9:9-13 and Luke 5:27-32). Jesus and his disciples are at table with a number of tax collectors and sinners (Mark notes that there were many such outcasts among his followers) and some scribes complain about the company Jesus is keeping. "Why," they ask, "do you eat and drink with tax collectors and sinners?" (Luke 5:30). Such friendship or solidarity with public sinners seems inappropriate for a prophet. Jesus answers that "Those who are well have no need of a physician, but those who are sick; I have come to call not the righteous but sinners to repentance" (Luke 5:31-32).

Jesus' radical table fellowship, then, is an offer of forgiveness and a call to repentance.[27] When he breaks bread with sinners and outcasts like Levi and the other tax collectors, Jesus is practicing and proclaiming the scandalously lavish mercy of God, a mercy reaching beyond all normal boundaries of friendship and table fellowship. Whatever their past offense, no sinner who is willing to repent will be denied this mercy or turned away from this table.

At the same time, while the offer of forgiveness is universal, so is the call to repentance. When Jesus eats with tax collectors and announces that he has not come to call the virtuous but sinners he is reminding us that all are sinners and all need to repent. Sinners are not a special class of people, but a universal condition. The only ones who will be able to sit down at table with Jesus, the only ones who will not be scandalized by this generous offer of forgiveness, are those who recognize their own sinfulness.

Jesus is again criticized for his table manners in Luke 7:36-50. Accepting a dinner invitation from a Pharisee named Simon, Jesus comes to his host's house to take his place at table. At some point in the meal an uninvited woman known to be a sinner comes and sits or kneels at Jesus' feet, weeping. Bathing his feet with her ample tears, she then wipes them dry with her hair, kisses them, and anoints them with a flask of myrrh.

Simon and his other guests are shocked by the woman's behavior and by Jesus' refusal to stop it. "If this man were a prophet," Simon thinks to himself, "he would have known who and what kind of woman this is who is touching him—that she is a sinner" (Luke 7:39). Those at table are even more troubled when Jesus tells this unclean woman that her sins are forgiven.

Here too a story of Jesus at table shows that God's offer of forgiveness and the need for repentance are both universal. As Jesus tells Simon, the only difference between him and this weeping woman is that she acknowledges and repents of her sinfulness. She has shown Jesus extraordinary gratitude because she has been forgiven much. But Simon, who thinks he has little to repent, offers little gratitude.

Mark's twin accounts of the miracle of the loaves and fishes (14:13-21; 15:32-39) provide other examples of Jesus' radical table fellowship with outcasts. In *Loaves and Fishes: The Gospel Feeding Narratives,* Joseph Grassi argues that Mark's first account has Jesus breaking and sharing bread with a Jewish crowd, while his second feeding miracle is described as taking place among the Gentiles. According to Grassi, Mark uses the twin accounts to show the early Church that "Jesus' mission was directed to . . . both Jews and Gentiles," and to indicate that their own Eucharistic community was to overcome any divisions between Jewish and Gentile disciples.[28] As Donald Senior notes, Mark was reminding the early Church that "Eucharistic table fellowship meant one bread for different peoples, just as Jesus . . . fed the hungry multitudes on both [the Jewish and Gentile] sides of the lake."[29]

In Luke's story of a meal in the house of Martha and Mary (10:38-42) Jesus is once again portrayed as a dinner guest who violates the cultural norms of his day. This time he has accepted hospitality at the home of a woman. Indeed, he "is spending time with two women who are not his relatives, having a woman serve him, and teaching a woman in her own house."[30] As Laverdiere notes, "that Martha welcomed Jesus into her home seems quite extraordinary. Ordinarily, a man would have been welcomed by a man into a man's home, but not by a woman into a woman's home."[31] By having these women host Jesus in their own home Luke presents Martha and Mary not only as friends and disciples of Jesus, but also as forerunners of the Christian women who would host the early Church in their homes. Jesus' radical table fellowship is being offered here as a model of a Eucharistic community where women and men are equals.

As we saw in our discussion of hospitality, Jesus also uses parables, particularly those about the heavenly banquet, to teach his disciples a radical table fellowship. In Luke 13:28-30, Jesus responds to a question about who will be saved by recounting a parable about guests at the banquet in the Kingdom of God. And in Luke 14:15-24 Jesus, a dinner guest in the home of a leading Pharisee, tells a story about those to be invited to "eat bread in the kingdom of God" (v. 15).

In both cases Jesus makes it clear that the friendship of God's table reaches far beyond those who expect to be the invited guests: "from east and west, from north and south, and will eat in the kingdom of God" (Luke 13:29). God will not only invite the poor, the crippled, the blind and the lame (who were often associated with sinners and social outcasts), but will also bring in those from "the roads and lanes" (Luke 14:23, a reference to Gentiles who lived outside the walls of Judaism). As Matthew 22:10 tells us in his version of the parable, God's servants will bring in "both good and bad." Indeed, sinners and outcasts will end up taking the honored places at God's table, because they have recognized their need for repentance and forgiveness.[32] As Jesus tells his audience in Matthew 21:31, "the tax collectors and the prostitutes are going into the kingdom of God ahead of you."

At Greco-Roman banquets those who broke bread together formed a friendship that included those at the table, but excluded those not deemed fit for an invitation. In his parables about the heavenly banquet, Jesus is telling his disciples that the friendship of God will not exclude any social outcasts or sinners who accept the invitation to repent and the offer of forgiveness. And he warns against the arrogance of the self-righteous who think themselves the only fit company at God's table, and rejects any divisions or fractions that divide the community according to social status, caste, race, or gender.

In Luke 15 Jesus is once again in the company of a large number of tax collectors and sinners, and the Pharisees and scribes are described as murmuring their disapproval that "This fellow welcomes sinners and eats with them" (v. 2). This time Jesus responds with three parables underscoring the reach of God's mercy and friendship. In the parables of the lost sheep (15:3-7), the lost coin (15:8-10), and the lost son (15:11-32) sinners are described as lost treasures or children for whom God zealously searches. And whenever God finds one of these lost sinners there is great rejoicing in heaven and on earth. When the shepherd finds the lost stray and the woman discovers her lost coin, both invite friends and neighbors to come and celebrate with them. And when the penitent son returns home, his parents kill the fatted calf and hold a great feast, "because this brother of yours was dead and has come to life; he was lost and has been found" (v. 32).

Finally, in Luke 19 we have the story of Jesus being welcomed into the house of Zacchaeus, a wealthy chief tax collector from Jericho. Seeing the great effort Zacchaeus has made to meet him, Jesus invites himself to the tax collector's home, once again provoking grumbling from the crowd that "He has gone to be the guest of one who is a sinner" (v. 7). This time, however, it is the repentant sinner who responds. Offering proof of his conversion, Zacchaeus acknowledges the monies he has extorted and promises to give half his wealth to the poor and to repay his theft four times over. Jesus blesses this repentant sinner with the announcement that "Today salvation has come to this house" (v. 9).

Again, the answer to the question about who can be saved or who will dine at the banquet in the kingdom of God is this: anyone who acknowledges their need for repentance and mercy. And anyone who fails to do this, or fails to show God's hospitality to other repentant sinners is unlikely to find a place at the table.

Friendship at the Eucharistic Table

As we saw earlier, the first disciples recognized and remembered Jesus in "the breaking of the bread" and sought in their Eucharistic communities to proclaim and practice the radical table fellowship of Jesus and the hospitality and friendship of the heavenly banquet. This hospitality not only obliged Christians to make room for the poor at their tables and in their homes, it also called them to befriend sinners and outcasts, and to overcome within their communities any fractions or divisions based on class, race, or gender.

Unlike the Greco-Roman banquets and symposia of their day, eucharistic celebrations were to welcome everyone, including women, children, and slaves. And they were to be open to Jews and Gentiles alike. As Eugene LaVerdiere notes, "When the Christians assembled for the breaking of the bread on the first day of the week, they assembled as a church. That meant the assembly was open to all, excluding no one by reason of race, sex, nationality, ethnic background, tribe, caste, social or economic status, or language."[33] Just as eucharistic hospitality demanded that there be no distinction between rich and poor at Christian assemblies or among Christians in general, so eucharistic friendship meant that there should be no divisions between "Jew or Greek, there is no longer slave or free, there is no longer male and female; for all of you are one in Christ Jesus" (Gal 3:28).

In Acts 6:1-7 we read of an early tension developing within the church in Jerusalem: "the Hellenists complained against the Hebrews because their widows were being neglected in the daily distribution of food" (v. 1). The eucharistic hospitality which had led these early Christians to share everything in common and ensure that there were no needy among them was now being distorted, and a distinction was being made based on language and culture.[34] This discrimination represented an unacceptable violation of the eucharistic friendship that defined this community as a church, and so the apostles gathered the whole community and appointed seven disciples "of good standing, full of the Spirit and of wisdom" (v. 3) to oversee the daily distribution and correct the problem.

A second test for the eucharistic friendship of the early Church involved welcoming and breaking bread with Gentiles. The first converts to Christianity were Jewish. Acts 2:1-41 reports that on Pentecost about 3,000 devout Jews of every nation were added to the number of believers. And in Acts 8:4-25 we learn that a number of Samaritans were also received into the Church. But until Cornelius, who is at the center of a story in Acts 10:1–11:18, there had been no Gentile converts. This was to be a critical turning point in the table fellowship of the Christian community.

The story begins in chapter 10 with an angel appearing to the centurion Cornelius and directing this devout and god-fearing Gentile to send for Simon Peter. Meanwhile, Peter has had his own vision, in which he has been instructed to eat foods considered unclean by Jewish dietary law. When Peter refuses, he is told three times that "What God has made clean, you must not call profane" (v. 15). Upon awakening from his trance Peter is escorted to Cornelius' house, where the apostle announces "God has shown me that I should not call anyone profane or unclean" (v. 28). And after admitting that "God shows no partiality" (v. 34) and that "in every nation anyone who fears him and does what is right is acceptable to him" (v. 35), Peter baptizes Cornelius and his whole household.

In chapter 11 Peter returns to Jerusalem and explains to those who have heard the news that God has indeed offered the Holy Spirit to the Gentiles and that faithful Christians must not stand in the Lord's way. Later, at the Council of Jerusalem (Acts 15:1-35) the early Church decides not to burden Gentile converts with Mosaic law regarding food and its preparation, thus removing a final barrier separating Jew and Gentile within the eucharistic community and allowing them to break bread together.

Eucharistic friendship also obliged Christians to overcome barriers and divisions between women and men, and the early Church did make some strides towards a radical table fellowship that befriended women as co-disciples, though much of this progress was later undone as the Church made accommodations to the larger culture.[35] As Karen Jo Torjesen notes in *When Women Were Priests,*

> Wherever Christianity spread, women were leaders of house churches. Mary, the mother of John Mark, presided over a house church in Jerusalem (Acts 12:12-17) . . . . Apphia presided over

two others in Colossae (Philem. 2). Nympha in Laodicea, Lydia in Thyatira, and Phoebe at Cenchrae supervised the congregations that met in their homes (Col 4:15, Acts 16:15, Rom 16:1).[36]

Present Challenges

The vision of Jesus' radical table fellowship and eucharistic friendship continues to challenge and haunt the Christian community. For breaking bread with one another at the Eucharist makes radical demands upon us, calling us to practice an inclusive table fellowship within our own assemblies and the world around us. To break this bread worthily we must address and overcome any fractions and divisions in our churches and societies, dismantling and reforming practices, structures, and systems that divide, exclude, or marginalize the outcasts who are our neighbors and companions. As Elizabeth Schüssler Fiorenza argues,

> The central symbol of the Christian association is not a code or a holy place, not a ritual formula or action, but the very concrete sharing of a meal in justice and love. The community gathered around the table of the Lord has to overcome its social stratifications and discriminations otherwise it makes itself guilty and answerable for 'profaning' the life and death of its Lord.[37]

We still have a long way to go in both our churches and the larger society before we can claim to be practicing the table fellowship of Jesus or the eucharistic friendship of the heavenly banquet. Many in our eucharistic assemblies and world are still treated as outcasts and sinners. Along with the gap between rich and poor our churches and societies are fractured by divisions based on gender and race.

Two thousand years after the early Church welcomed women as companions and ministers at the eucharistic table, Christianity continues to suffer from the social sins of sexism and patriarchy. Our own Catholic community clings to sexist language in its public worship and argues that only males are fit representatives of Jesus at the Eucharist. Women are excluded from preaching, celebrating the sacraments, and any key roles of leadership, and—unlike men—continue to be defined largely in terms of their reproductive roles. We have a very long way to go before it can be said of our churches that there is neither male nor female, for we are all one in Christ.

Nor is the picture much better outside our church walls: as J. Milburne Thompson notes in *Justice and Peace: A Christian Primer,* "Sexism is characteristic of every society and culture on earth . . . [and] though some nations have made significant progress toward the goal of gender equality, no society has reached that goal."[38] No society treats women as well as men. Women are more likely to be hungry, poor, and uneducated, less likely to be promoted, elected, or provided with adequate medical care. Anne Carr notes in an essay on women and justice that "women are one half of the world's population, work two-thirds of the world's work-hours, receive one-tenth of the world's income and own less than 1/100 of the world's property."[39] And in every society, class, and community women suffer from a plague of sexual and domestic violence that will leave half of them battered at least once before they die.

Race too fractures our eucharistic communities. Although enforced segregation has disappeared from Christian Churches in the U.S., our congregations remain largely separate and unequal when it comes to color. Recent studies indicate that "only about 10% of the congregations in the United States are integrated or interracial."[40] As Kenneth Himes notes,

> In a nation where housing is still largely segregated, the decline of the large urban parish has led to further racial division in the Christian community as whites worship in suburban isolation from blacks. Our worshiping communities too often reflect rather than challenge the *de facto* apartheid of our nation.[41]

And though our nation and society have made some real progress in race relations, blacks and other minorities continue to experience discrimination in the workplace and housing market. Over the past three decades the income gap between whites and blacks has grown, not shrunk, and huge numbers of young black men have been imprisoned as the result of a drug war that targets low-income neighborhoods. Race continues to matter in our society.

At the Eucharist we break bread in memory of the radical table fellowship of Jesus and in anticipation of the eucharistic friendship of the heavenly banquet. For too long most of us have been unconscious of the implications of this breaking of the bread, unaware of the demands of this table. William Crockett points out that

Jesus' eating with outcasts and sinners was a sign of God's invitation to the outcast to share in the banquet table of the kingdom. Jesus' proclamation and activity breaks down social barriers and is a sign of the offer of participation in the coming reign of God to those who have been marginalized by society.[42]

If we are to break this bread worthily, we need to practice a eucharistic friendship that overcomes divisions between Jew and Greek, slave and free, male and female.

Service: Dismantling Hierarchies

A Sign of Contradiction

Breaking bread with others is a sign of communion, solidarity, and friendship and a recognition of the common dignity and worth of those with whom we eat. When we share a meal of bread and wine we celebrate and reinforce the basic bonds and moral ties that connect us to one another and acknowledge our fundamental equality as persons. No longer strangers, enemies, or servants we become companions and friends.

Still, bread and wine have also been signs of division, oppression, and injustice, and our meals together have celebrated and reinforced structures of alienation and marginalization. Bread and wine are agricultural products, and the birth of agriculture led to the rise of hierarchical societies and empires divided between the many who worked the land and the few who ate the first fruits of these labors.

As we saw in chapter 1, before the development of agriculture about 10,000 years ago, humans lived in small bands of hunter-gatherers who shared both the work of collecting and preparing food and the food itself in a fairly egalitarian manner. The invention of agriculture led to a division between those who owned the land (and thus the food) and those who did not, and allowed a small elite class of non-farmers to extract their food from masses of slaves, peasants, and serfs.[43] What's more, societies and regions with the good fortune to develop agriculture first were able to dominate or decimate peoples who lagged behind. The first peoples to grow crops were usually also the first to raise armies and build empires. Europe's colonization and oppression of Africa, Asia, and the Americas was in no small way a result of the fact that the people of the Fertile Crescent were able to grow crops before those in other regions of the planet.[44] Thus the capacity to make bread and wine (and other agricultural products) went hand in hand with the rise of stratified and hierarchical societies that drew lines of division between master and slave, oppressor and oppressed.

We saw earlier that even today those who labor to produce and provide our daily bread are paid and respected less than those who have their food prepared for them. Those who pick, pack, and process our food, as well as those who wait on our tables are usually drawn from the ranks of the poor and lower class. They are mostly minorities, immigrants, and/or women. The middle class and wealthy rarely want their children to grow up to be food servers. We are as deeply divided by our ties to food as we are united by them.

And these divisions and injustices have long been played out in the liturgies of our meals. Alongside the friendship and companionship of dinner guests who treat one another as peers and equals has been a table or meal hierarchy separating master and servant, rich and poor, male and female. In the common meal or Greco-Roman banquet tradition of the ancient Mediterranean world there was a general sense of equality among dinner guests. But, as in George Orwell's *Animal Farm,* some were clearly more equal than others, and a ranked seating arrangement reflected and reinforced this hierarchy of diners. Still, an even deeper chasm separated the free men who reclined on couches and the women and servants who might occasionally sit with them, but were more generally excluded from this company, joining the dinner only to wait upon the guests or provide some entertainment.[45]

In societies and homes where there were no servants or slaves, there were still women. Indeed, there are few places where the drama of patriarchy's domination and oppression of women has been more clearly and consistently acted out than at the dinner table. Across cultures and down through the centuries women have been expected to prepare and serve men's meals, to wait upon men, to wash up before and after them, to eat after them, and to take a lower place at table.[46] With some exceptions, table service has been women's work. It has been the woman's role to set the table, cook the meal, and clean up after it. And it has been the man's role to be waited upon, to be fed, and to receive deference. The intimate communion of the domestic meal has been distorted by sexist structures of oppression and injustice.

It is at all these hierarchies that Jesus' radical table fellowship takes such sharp and deadly aim. Along with proclaiming and practicing a hospitality that makes room for the poor and a friendship that welcomes sinners and outcasts, Jesus embraces a table service that forsakes the honored place at dinner, takes a seat with the lowly, and picks up a basin and towel to wash the feet of dinner guests (see John 13:3-16). In this way he is challenging not just what happens at mealtime, but all of the embedded structures and practices that create and protect privilege and power for elite groups of every sort. To counteract a table hierarchy that celebrates and perpetuates inequality (political, economic, social), oppression, and injustice, Jesus demands that his disciples take the lowest place at table, not merely the lowest place for a guest, but the place of those invisible and oppressed women and men who serve.

Jesus' Table Service

In Mark 9:33-37 Jesus challenges the hierarchy of the world with the hierarchy of God's heavenly banquet.[47] His disciples have been arguing among themselves about which of them is the greatest, just as guests at a dinner might squabble about who deserves the highest place at table. Jesus responds by explaining the "lower-archy" he has come to proclaim and practice, the table service of God's heavenly banquet. "Whoever wants to be first," Jesus tells them, "must be last of all and servant of all" (v. 35). That is, the greatest one at God's table will not just take the lowest seat available to a guest, but will assume the role of servant, waiting on table and eating after all the guests are served. This is a complete reversal of the disciples' expectations and of the world's table manners.

Then Jesus takes a child and putting his arms around the toddler announces that "Whoever welcomes one such child in my name welcomes me, and whoever welcomes me welcomes not me but the one who sent me" (v. 37). Children had no place at the Greco-Roman banquet or formal dinner, and Jesus offers one of these little ones as an example of all the lowly, poor, and oppressed who are excluded from the world's tables or pressed into the service of its guests. As he does in the parable of the last judgment in Matthew 25, Jesus announces that he is one of these "little ones," and that if we welcome the world's lowly and discarded, we are welcoming Jesus, and the One who has sent Jesus. Again, the one who is the host of the heavenly banquet identifies with those considered too lowly to be guests at our tables.

In Luke 14:7-11 Jesus repeats his advice about table service to a larger audience. At a leading Pharisee's house for dinner, Jesus notices that his fellow guests are jockeying for the places of honor at table and tells them a parable about guests at a wedding feast. When invited to such a feast they should not take one of the honored seats, for this may be reserved for a more important guest, and they would be humiliated to be asked to give up their seat. Instead, they should take the lowest place, and when their host invites them to come up higher, they will be well thought of by all.

Given what Jesus has told his disciples elsewhere, this parable about the wedding feast should not be seen as advice on how to avoid embarrassment or garner praise. Rather, it is a call to practice a table fellowship that reverses and dismantles the hierarchies that divide master and slave, male and female, rich and poor, and shows solidarity with those at the bottom of these hierarchies. Like the call to turn one's cheek and go the extra mile, the challenge to take the lowest place is an invitation to resist structures of oppression and injustice by refusing to cooperate. Taking the lowest seat is a form of nonviolent resistance to all these hierarchies and a practice that anticipates a heavenly banquet where such divisions have been overcome.

Another Lukan parable (12:33-37) reinforces this image of the heavenly banquet as a table at which all our present hierarchies have been dismantled. As Joseph Grassi notes, "Jesus instructs his disciples to be like servants ready to receive their master and serve him when he returns from a wedding feast. An unimaginable surprise happens when the master returns. He girds himself as a slave and begins to personally serve his servants instead."[48] In this incredible reversal of roles the host of the heavenly banquet has taken on the identity of a servant and is waiting upon the servants of the household, practicing a table service that undoes every type of oppression and marginalization. This startling behavior anticipates Jesus' announcement at the Last Supper that he is among them like a servant (Luke 22:27), and his own washing of the disciples' feet (John 13:3-16) reveals a God who does not tolerate the world's hierarchies.

As we saw earlier, the miracle of the loaves and fishes provides Jesus' disciples with an opportunity to practice his table service. In the various accounts of this feeding miracle it is the task of the disciples to give the hungry crowd something to eat. They are to bring the food to Jesus and it is their task to distribute the meal to the thousands of children, women, and men seated in this lonely place. Later, when all have had their fill, it falls to the disciples to gather up the remnants in baskets. In each of these tasks they have played the servant's role and offer readers a model of the sort of servant-disciple Jesus calls us all to be.

Still, the lesson of table service is a hard one to learn. In several places in Matthew the disciples of Jesus continue to be obsessed with privilege and rank, hoping to secure the places of honor and positions of advantage over one another.[49] Even in the Last Supper account in Luke 22:25-27, Jesus is confronted with a dispute among his followers about which of them should be considered the greatest. Again, Jesus responds by offering a model of table service that will completely reverse the political and economic hierarchies of their world. "The kings of the Gentiles lord it over them; and those in authority over them are called benefactors. But not so with you; rather the greatest among you must become like the youngest, and the leader like one who serves" (vv. 25-26).

Certainly the most striking example of Jesus' radical table service comes in John's account of the Last Supper (13:1-30).[50] "Jesus . . . got up from the table, took off his outer robe, and tied a towel around himself. Then he poured water into a basin and began to wash the disciples' feet and to wipe them with the towel that was tied around him" (vv. 3-5). Peter, who is scandalized by this outrageous behavior, announces that he will never allow Jesus to wash his feet. But Jesus informs his wary disciple that unless he cooperates and indeed imitates this service there will be no communion or table fellowship between them. And then he tells his dinner companions twice that they are to do what he has done: "[I]f I, your Lord and Teacher, have washed your feet, you also ought to wash one another's feet. For I have set you an example, that you also should do as I have done to you" (vv. 14-15).

At the heart of the other accounts of the Last Supper is the breaking of the bread. When Jesus breaks bread with his disciples he is practicing and proclaiming God's heavenly banquet, inviting his disciples to join him as companions at that table, and commanding them to practice a radical table fellowship that overcomes boundaries between Jew and Greek, master and slave, male and female. "Do this in memory of me," he tells them. In John's account this stunning act of service is the sign of the heavenly banquet and the behavior the friends and dinner companions of Jesus are to imitate. The lord and master of the house, the one who should be blessing and breaking the bread, has gotten up from the highest place at table and slipped into the role of servant, washing their feet like a common slave.

When Christians celebrate the Eucharist they are not just called to remember and recognize Christ in the breaking of the bread and to practice the hospitality and friendship of Jesus' radical table fellowship. They are also commanded to get up from their seat, gird themselves as servants, and wait on table—overturning every hierarchy of power, prestige, and advantage. Celebrating the Eucharist means dismantling every structure of oppression, injustice, and marginalization.

Eucharistic Table Service

We have already seen that the Eucharistic community of the early Church understood itself as called to practice Jesus' table service. In Acts 6:1-6 we read that the apostles themselves had the task of waiting on tables for the widows and other poor in the community. They were responsible for the daily distribution of food to those in need in the Church, just as Jesus had assigned them the role as servants in the various accounts of the miracle of the loaves and fishes. And when the number of believers grew too large for this task to be handled by the Twelve, the community selected and ordained seven disciples "full of the Spirit and of wisdom," who were ordained for this ministry.

So too the author of James (2:1-7) warns his Christian audience against perpetuating hierarchies that offer the honored places to those with wealth and power, and force the poor to stand in the corner or sit on the floor by one of the other guest's footstool. If anyone is to be shown special preference in Christian assemblies and gatherings it is those who are poor and lowly in the eyes of the world. In a similar fashion the passage in the *Didascalia apostolorum* noted above instructs the bishop to welcome any poor person who comes into the Eucharistic assembly by getting up and offering that person his or her own place, even if this means that the bishop is to sit on the floor.[51]

Present Challenges

Practicing and imitating the table service modeled and proclaimed by Jesus challenges those who break bread at the Eucharist to dismantle hierarchies separating master and slave, rich and poor, male and female. Those who call themselves the friends and dinner companions of Christ cannot engage in disputes about places of honor but must instead refuse to cooperate in economic, political, and ecclesiastical structures of oppression, inequality, and injustice. As Monika Hellwig has written, the "Eucharist fails of its purpose if it reflects discrimination between rich and poor such as exists in the larger society. Christian faith and practice are incompatible with arrogant claims to special status and privilege, and with maintenance of factions and discrimination."[52] Elizabeth Schüssler Fiorenza puts it even more strongly:

> *All* Christians must be able to participate equally in the table-community of the one Body. Social discriminations destroy the tablecommunity of the Lord's Supper. The sharing of all members of the Christian association—rich and poor, free and slave, men and women, Jews and Greeks—in the one broken bread constitutes the one body, the ecclesia. The becoming of Church as well as the symbolic ritualisation of Church, is not possible without equality in actual tablesharing. However, equal tablesharing requires the abandoning of societal discriminations among those who partake in the Body and Blood of Christ.[53]

In the Eucharist we are called to celebrate a meal that remembers and imitates the table service of Jesus and anticipates the table service of God's heavenly banquet. At the table of the Last Supper, Jesus offers us a practice where servants have been transformed into friends and where masters have become servants. Unlike the table or meal hierarchy that it challenges and seeks to dismantle, the communion and fellowship of this meal is not based on slavery, oppression, or patriarchy. It does not need a class of servants or maids to sustain its island of friendship or equality. The collegiality of the few is not based on the servitude of the many.

We are still a long way from this radical table service. We have not yet achieved full equality or friendship in our churches, homes, or world, and the bread we break at our tables is leavened with a good deal of injustice and oppression. As we have noted throughout this chapter, class, gender, and race continue to divide our communities and churches. Thousands of years after the Hebrew prophets said that authentic worship meant justice for the poor, the widowed, and the aliens, these three groups still make up the bottom ranks of our political, economic, and ecclesiastical hierarchies.

Still, the most enduring and glaring failure of eucharistic table service has been Christianity and Catholicism's inability to overcome the chasm separating women and men at the eucharistic table. The unwillingness to abandon a sexist table hierarchy in our ritual and sacramental celebration of Jesus' table fellowship keeps us from fulfilling his command to "do this in memory of me." In a church where only men can preside at Eucharist, say the blessing over the bread we break, or take the honored seats at liturgy, the sign of a male priest bending down to wash parishioners feet once a year is tragically muted, even eviscerated. And the maintenance of a patriarchal table at the Eucharist out of a misguided belief that males can more adequately image Jesus results in a meal that distorts the image of the heavenly banquet that Jesus practiced and proclaimed. Beggars, tax collectors, Gentiles, and sinners of every sort are to be welcomed at God's banquet, and they will be given the honored seats. But at our Eucharist women are still fit only to wait upon the men. We cannot have a church where only half the congregation is expected to follow Jesus' command to play the servant.

Conclusion

In the Eucharist we practice and proclaim the table fellowship of Jesus and anticipate the table fellowship of God's heavenly banquet. This radical table fellowship makes us a church and forms us into disciples and companions of Jesus. It teaches us a set of Christian "manners" about hospitality, friendship, and service. Radical table fellowship calls us to make room for the poor, welcome outcasts and sinners, and take a seat with the lowly. Practicing these table manners puts us in tension with political, economic, and ecclesiastical hierarchies that divide our tables, separating master and servant, rich and poor, male and female. And it places us in solidarity with those who have been excluded from our common tables or pressed into service at them. After two millennia, our eucharistic celebrations continue to be imperfect images of Jesus' table service and offer a view of the heavenly banquet as if seen through a "mirror, dimly" (1 Cor 13:12). Still, the beacon of Jesus' radical table fellowship calls us to approach more closely the banquet being prepared for all.

Notes

[1] Eugene LaVerdiere, *The Breaking of the Bread: The Development of the Eucharist According to the Acts of the Apostles* (Chicago: Liturgical Training Publications, 1998) 7–35.

[2] Dennis E. Smith, "The Historical Jesus at Table," *Society of Biblical Literature* (Atlanta: Scholars Press, 1989) 474–84.

[3] Dennis E. Smith and Hal E. Taussig, *Many Tables: The Eucharist in the New Testament and Liturgy Today* (Philadelphia: Trinity Press, 1990) 23–28.

[4] Eugene LaVerdiere, *Dining in the Kingdom of God: The Origins of the Eucharist According to Luke* (Chicago: Liturgy Training Publications, 1994) 16–21.

[5] Gillian Feeley-Harnik, *The Lord's Table: Eucharist and Passover in Early Christianity* (Philadelphia: University of Pennsylvania Press, 1981) 130–45.

[6] Christine D. Pohl, *Making Room: Recovering Hospitality as a Christian Tradition* (Grand Rapids, Mich.: Eerdmans, 1999) 3–6.

[7] Pohl, *Making Room*, 17.

[8] LaVerdiere, *The Breaking of the Bread*, 86.

[9] Pohl, *Making Room*, 33.

[10] Lactantius, *The Divine Institutions,* bk. 6, chap. 12, in *The Ante-Nicene Fathers,* vol. 7, ed. Alexander Roberts and James Donaldson (Edinburgh: T & T Clark, 1867–1872) 176.

[11] Jerome, Letter 52: "To Nepotian," in *Select Letters of Jerome,* with English trans. F. A. Wright, The Loeb Classical Library [Latin Authors], (Cambridge, Mass.: Harvard University Press, 1975) 217–19.

[12] Justin Martyr, *1 Apology*, 67.7, cited in William R. Crockett, *Eucharist: Symbol of Transformation* (New York: Pueblo, 1989) 255.

[13] *Didascalia Apostolorum* 12, cited in Crockett, *Symbol of Transformation*, 255.

[14] John J. Mitchell, *Critical Voices in American Catholic Economic Thought* (New York: Paulist, 1989) 77–105.

[15] Ibid., 130–52; Paul Hanley Furfey, "Liturgy and the Social Problem," in *National Liturgical Week: Held at the Cathedral of St. Paul and the Catholic Youth Center, St. Paul, Minnesota, October 6–10, 1941* (Newark, N.J.: Benedictine Liturgical Conference, 1942) 181–86.

[16] Mitchell, *Critical Voices*, 106–29; 153–73.

[17] Editorial, "The Unglobal Economy," *Canada & the World Backgrounder,* September 2001, 19–20; Richard W. Stevenson, "Study Details Income Gap between Rich and the Poor," *New York Times,* 31 May 2001, sec. C.

[18] Patrick T. McCormick, "Sacred Space: Balancing the Sanctuary and the Commons," *Worship* 74 (2000) 42–44.

[19] Paul A. Jargowsky, *Poverty and Place: Ghettos, Barrios, and the American City* (New York: Russell Sage, 1997) 31–33; Edward J. Blakely and Mary Gail Snyder, *Fortress America: Gated Communities in the United States* (Washington, D.C.: Brookings Institution, 1997).

[20] Patrick T. McCormick, "Just Punishment and America's Prison Experiment," *Theological Studies* 61 (2000) 508–32.

[21] David Quammen, "Planet of Weeds," *Harper's,* October 1998, 61, 65.

[22] Kenneth R. Himes, "Eucharist and Justice: Assessing the Legacy of Virgil Michel," *Worship* 62 (1988) 219.

[23] Philippe Rouillard, "From Human Meal to Christian Eucharist: II," *Worship* 53 (1979) 47.

[24] Smith and Taussig, *Many Tables,* 21–23.

[25] Cited in Dennis Smith, "Table Fellowship as a Literary Motif in the Gospel of Luke," *Journal of Biblical Literature* 106 (1987) 634.

[26] Smith, "Table Fellowship," 634.

[27] LaVerdiere, *Dining in the Kingdom of God,* 36–42.

[28] Grassi, *Loaves and Fishes,* 26.

[29] Donald Senior, "The Eucharist in Mark: Mission, Reconciliation, Hope," *Biblical Theology Bulletin* 12 (1982) 69.

[30] Robert J. Karris, "The Gospel According to Luke," in *The New Jerome Biblical Commentary,* ed. Raymond E. Brown, S.S.; Joseph A. Fitzmyer, S.J.; and Roland E. Murphy, O. Carm. (Englewood Cliffs, N.J.: Prentice Hall, 1990) 702.

[31] LaVerdiere, *Dining in the Kingdom of God,* 81.

[32] Feeley-Harnik, *The Lord's Table,* 110.

[33] LaVerdiere, *The Breaking of the Bread,* 94.

[34] Ibid., 111–25.

[35] Raymond F. Collins, *Sexual Ethics and the New Testament: Behavior and Belief* (New York: Herder & Herder, 2000) 186–87; Lisa Sowle Cahill, *Sex, Gender and Christian Ethics* (New York: Cambridge University Press, 1996) 150–60.

[36] Karen Jo Torjesen, *When Women Were Priests: Women's Leadership in the Early Church & the Scandal of their Subordination in the Rise of Christianity* (San Francisco: HarperSanFrancisco, 1993) 33.

[37] Elisabeth Schüssler Fiorenza, "Tablesharing and the Celebration of the Eucharist," in *Can We Always Celebrate the Eucharist?* Ed. Mary Collins and David Power, Concilium (New York) 152 (New York: Seabury Press, 1982) 10.

[38] J. Milburne Thompson, *Justice and Peace: A Christian Primer* (Maryknoll, N.Y.: Orbis, 1997) 98.

[39] Anne Carr, "Women, Justice, and the Church," *Horizons* 17 (1990) 275.

[40] Sheilia Hardwell Byrd, "Churches Seek to Bridge Racial Divide," *Columbian (Clark County, Washington),* 1 July 2000, sec. E.

[41] Himes, "Eucharist and Justice," 219.

[42] Crockett, *Symbol of Transformation,* 253.

[43] Clive Ponting, *A Green History of the World: The Environment and the Collapse of Great Civilizations* (New York: Penguin, 1991) 52–55; Jared Diamond, *Guns, Germs and Steel: The Fates of Human Societies* (New York: W. W. Norton, 1997) 265–92.

[44] Diamond, *Guns, Germs and Steel,* 85–103.

[45] Smith, *Many Tables,* 30–35.

[46] Gillian Feeley-Harnik, "Religion and Food: An Anthropological Perspective," *Journal of the American Academy of Religion* 63 (1995) 575.

[47] See also Luke 9:46-48 and Matt 18:1-5; 20:20-28; 23:6-12.

[48] Grassi, *Loaves and Fishes,* 78.

[49] Matthew 18:1-5; 20:20-28; 23:6-12.

[50] R. Kevin Seasoltz, "Justice and the Eucharist," *Worship* 58 (1984) 507–25.

[51] *Didascalia apostolorum* 12, cited in Crockett, *Symbol of Transformation,* 255.

[52] Monika Hellwig, *The Eucharist and the Hunger of the World,* rev. ed. (Kansas City, Mo.: Sheed & Ward, 1992) 19.

[53] Schüssler Fiorenza, "Tablesharing and the Celebration of the Eucharist," 11.

Chapter Three

"This Is My Body"

Recognizing the Body of Christ

"This is my body." We hear these words every Sunday as we pray in the Eucharist that the bread and wine we offer and share might "become for us the body and blood of Jesus Christ." This prayer expresses our faith that the risen Christ is really and sacramentally present to us in this eucharistic meal. In this bread, blessed, broken, and shared we recognize and participate in the real presence, the Body of Christ. At the same time we pray in the Eucharist not just that the food we offer might be transformed into Christ's body, but also that we, the community of disciples gathered around the table, will become more fully that which we are—the Body of Christ. For Paul tells us that "Now you are the body of Christ and individually members of it" (1 Cor 12:27). In baptism we have died with Christ and been born again in Christ. And so in the Eucharist we, the Church, celebrate our own identity and vocation as the Body of Christ—recognizing the real presence of Christ in the meal being shared and in the community sharing and being nurtured and shaped by that meal. Recognizing ourselves as the Body of Christ means acknowledging that our baptism has joined us to Christ and tied us to one another. We are now one, and old divisions, hostilities, and inequalities must dissolve in this new union. This same union also calls us to care for the wounded and broken parts of Christ's body. Discerning the Body of Christ, then, means seeing Christ present in the bread broken and shared, in the whole community formed and sustained by that sharing, and in the bodies of the sick, suffering, hungry, naked, imprisoned, and dying. We will know that we are the Body of Christ when we honor all the members of Christ's body and show special care for those bodies of Christ crying out in pain and suffering. This is the sort of body we pray to be transformed into, asking that we may become for others the Body of Christ.

After the death of Jesus of Nazareth the disciples discovered that his tomb was empty and his corpse missing. But in the days and weeks that followed many witnesses testified that they had encountered the risen Christ, and that Christ had been bodily present to them, eating and talking with them, even being touched by them. This was no phantom or imagined spirit, but a real person. God had raised Jesus from the dead, and Christ was now among them in a radically new and transformed way. The Body of Christ had been freed of all the shackles of death and sin, all the limits of time and space. And this transformation of Christ's body meant that all who were joined to it would also join in his resurrection.

Along with these early encounters with the risen Christ, the first disciples also came to recognize the Body of Christ in the breaking of the bread, and came to see that in baptism they had died with Christ and were taken up into to his new and resurrected body. In the Eucharist, Christians recognized the Body of Christ and re-membered themselves to that risen body. In the Eucharist they celebrated their baptismal identity and vocation as members of the Body of Christ. Being one body in Christ meant that they were now part of one another and that their communion in Christ made it impossible for them to sustain the divisions that had separated them into different bodies. There could no longer be distinctions between Jew and Greek, slave and free, male and female. Neither the bodily mark of circumcision nor the embodied differences of race, class, or gender could divide them any longer. Nor could they ignore or overlook the bodily needs and sufferings of their neighbors. Being one body meant paying attention to the hungers of the poor and the cries of the oppressed. So the eucharistic community of Acts that broke bread together made certain that the bodies of all were attended to in their needs.

In the Eucharist each Sunday we proclaim that "this is my body which will be given up for you." With this proclamation we affirm that Christ is really present in the bread blessed, broken, and shared, that we the community of baptized gathered around this table are one body in Christ, and that we are called to be the Body of Christ for others. Being the Body of Christ means honoring all the members of Christ and showing special care for those wounded and broken limbs and organs of Christ's body who are our sick, suffering, hungry, poor, and oppressed neighbors. "This is my body."

What It Means to Be Somebody

In the chapter on the eucharistic command to "take and eat" we asked what it means to be an eater, and in the chapter on breaking bread we asked what it means to sit down at table with others. Here in this chapter on the Eucharist and the Body of Christ we need to stop and ask ourselves what it means to *be* a body. If we are going to explore the moral implications of the Eucharist and Church as the Body of Christ we need to have a clear idea about our own bodies and bodiliness. We need to take a long, loving look at our own bodies and embodiment.

Our question here is what it means to *be* a body, not to *have* a body. Asking the question this way reminds us that we are embodied persons; not just spirits or souls that possess, inhabit, or find ourselves trapped in bodies. We *are* our bodies. We are somebodies. Wound our flesh, break our limbs, press our backs into servitude and you harm *us*. Fill our empty stomachs, slake our thirst, or mop our fevered brow and you give *us* comfort. Our bodies are not each a vestment or a vessel; they are part and parcel of our humanity. In *The Merchant of Venice* (3.1.50–69) Shylock rails against the anti-Semitic bigotry of Christians by crying out that he is a *somebody*. "Hath not a Jew eyes? Hath not a Jew hands, organs, dimensions, or senses?" Are Jews not "fed with the same food, hurt with the same weapons, subject to the same diseases, healed by the same means, warmed and cooled by the same winter and summer? If you prick us, do *we* not bleed? If you tickle us, do *we* not laugh? If you poison us, do *we* not die?"[1] Shylock's argument is that he is a *somebody* just like them, that he and they share the same flesh, and that the inhumanity of his Christian neighbors is found in the fact that they treat him as a *nobody*.

What does it mean, then, to be a body, to be somebody? Not to be an ethereal spirit or an abstract idea, but to be a body in a universe full of bodies? First, of course, it means to be physical, material, and concrete. It means to be made of matter or stuff, to be composed of atomic or subatomic particles, to have mass, extension, and volume. Even more, it means to be made of some particular stuff, some specific arrangement of quarks, atoms, molecules, compounds, or cells. Being a body means being *this* body and not *that* body; it means taking up a particular space, having a very definite shape, crowding out anything else that might have been in that space, and being hemmed in by everything at the edges of that space. It means being located in a par-ticular point in time, and changing or remaining the same as time moves on. Being a body means being subject to all the laws and forces of physics, chemistry, and (for living bodies) biology: having to share space with and make room for other bodies—acting and being acted on by other bodies—near and far.

Being a body also means being related to all the other bodies in the universe and to the huge body of the cosmos. As feminist theolo-gian Beverly Wildung Harrison has written, "The body-self is the integrated locus of our being in the world. We are related to every-thing through our body-selves: our bodies ground our connection to the world. Our bodies are the vehicles of relation that put us in touch with reality at every level."[2] From quarks to galaxies, from plankton to planets, every body in the universe is woven into the fabric of the cosmos and tied to every other body by a common heritage and makeup. Though each of our stories and structures are distinct, we all ultimately come from the same original moment and are fashioned of the same stuff. The oldest galaxy and the newest snowflake can trace their roots back to the creation of the universe and are built of the matter that originated in that first instant. And all of these bodies are in relationship to one another and to the whole cosmic harmony that makes up the universe. A snowflake landing on the eastern slopes of the Andes could be a cause or consequence of a drought in China or the collapse of a star at the edge of the Milky Way. Being somebody means being a body within the larger and interconnected body of the universe and being subject to all the balancing forces operating in that universe—and companion or neighbor to every other body that moves or rests within that body. Thus, what we do as bodies is important not just for ourselves, but for all the other bodies (large and small) that are impacted and shaped by our acts.

And if being a body makes us cousins and companions of every comet, quasar, and cloud, being a living body ties us even more closely to all the other life forms on the planet. Every organism, from the giant sequoia to the infinitesimal protozoan, is built of cells that could pass for siblings under the microscope. We all have genes and DNA that are amazingly similar and operate in basically the same way. We all interact with and depend on our local and larger environments, trying to find or create some niche or place where we can secure the food, space, and security we need to survive and flourish. We all need to metabolize food from our environment, transforming some carbon-based material into a part of our bodies and providing us with the energy to grow, work, rest, repair, or reproduce. And we all begin eventually to break down and die, leaving behind the stuff with which other living bodies will feed, fuel, and fashion themselves. From the chrysanthemum to the chimpanzee the family resemblance is striking.

But our connection to other living bodies is not just that we look or operate like them. Being a living body means that we need and depend on other bodies, and that we must find our place in the vast and vital ecosystem of creation. Our bodies are not separate, independent atoms, or self-contained units with rigid, inflexible boundaries. We are not islands. Instead, our bodies are woven into a living tapestry of organisms that feeds and protects its members by sharing, complementing, and recycling the differing gifts, talents, and flesh of all its hosts. In many large rainforest-trees, colonies of insects, animals, and plants sustain and nurture themselves, and one another, in a symphony of symbiosis. So too in the larger environment all living bodies must cooperate with and rely on one another to secure the food, water, light, shelter, and security they need to exist. And for highly complex living organisms like humans, being somebody means being particularly dependent on the huge array of bacteria, plants, and animals that clean our air, moderate our weather, pollinate our crops, enrich our soil, and provide our food, clothing, shelter, and medicines.

Being somebody also connects us with all other human bodies. At our conception we are knitted of the flesh and bodies of our parents and their parents, borrowing our genes and DNA from them. Growing up we discover that we have our mother's eyes and height, our father's chin and musical ear, or our grandmother's slender fingers. And the similarities reach beyond family and tribe, tying us to the larger human community and all the faces and bodies we see in *National Geographic* and every human body since we first began to walk upright. As Shylock argues, whether Jew or Greek, black or white, male or female, we all have the same flesh, are wounded by the same injuries, and comforted by the same pleasures. All of us are special, but none of us is immortal or invincible, or fashioned of a different clay or DNA than our first parents. To be somebody is to be related to and like every other somebody. It is to be peer and neighbor to every other body, whether sick or healthy, young or old, weak or strong. It is to know that every limit, wound, injury, or frailty that age or illness or misfortune has inscribed on the flesh of another could (and may someday) be inscribed on our own.

And to be somebody is to rest on the shoulders of other human bodies. As fetuses and newborns our need for other bodies is pervasive, intense, and undeniable. If we are taken away from the bodies that hold and care for us we cease to flourish and begin to die. In our infancy we are carried and nursed by other bodies, washed and fed, clothed and sheltered by other hands and arms, and provided for by the sweat of other brows. Other ears hear our cries and other fingers wipe away our tears. When we are children other bodies teach us to talk, walk, read, work, play, pray, sing, and dance. And even when we are fully grown and think of ourselves as standing on our own two feet, other bodies plant, pick, or prepare our food, build our roads or homes, protect our streets and children, and caress and hold us in the night. Indeed, every part of human civilization, every discovery, development, invention, construction, and convenience was birthed through the labor and genius of other bodies. And when we have grown sick or old, other bodies mop our fevered brows and nurse our wounds, carry our loads, hold our trembling hands, and prepare us for the journey home. To be somebody is to depend on the labor and love of thousands of other bodies. It takes a village to bear a body.

To be somebody is also to be sensual and symbolic, to know and love the world *as* bodies. Unlike angels or phantoms, our knowledge of ourselves and the world is embodied. It has been inscribed on our flesh, written on the tablet of our senses. We know and are known not as spirits, but as bodies that feel the world's blessing and burdens, pleasures and pains, bodies that are moved by the wonder and majesty of creation, saddened by the suffering of neighbors, and sickened by the face of cruelty. We have touched, tasted, smelled, heard, and seen the world, and we have come to know and understand it and ourselves from the sensual conversation our bodies have had with other bodies. Everything we know or believe or feel we know or believe or feel *as* bodies. Even our abstract notions are borne of and shaped by our bodily experience. Friendship and love are the comfort of a warm and steady embrace, the stroke of a gentle hand. Injustice is the savage sting of the taskmaster's whip or the torturer's prod. Illness is the nausea of an unsteady stomach, the ache of swelling joints, a night of fevered and fragile sleep. And our capacity (even as we read this passage) to imagine, to sympathize with the sufferings and injuries of others different or distant from ourselves comes from our ability to know these experiences by turning to our own bodily knowledge.

And so we make ourselves known through our bodies. We reach out to others, trying to communicate our embodied experience and knowledge through the sacraments of our language, gestures, symbols, and rituals. We seek to express our love in a steady gaze, a warm embrace, a caress, a sonnet, or a rose. We celebrate our communion by sitting down at a table, breaking bread, and sharing a cup of wine. We offer our blessing or care for the sick by rocking their aching and fevered bodies in our arms, or anointing head and hands with scented oil. Our communion with other bodies is fashioned of this vocabulary of symbols bearing our embodied experience and knowledge to one another and trying to fashion some fuller knowing of each other. To be somebody is to have only our bodies to know and be known, to love and be loved.

Being a body also means being limited, frail, and powerless—or at least not powerful enough to have or do all we wish. In spite of all of our prowess, vigor, and talents, regardless of our wondrous gifts and accomplishments and alongside our deepest pleasures and ecstasies, being somebody means being mortal. We bruise and break, grow old and sick and frail. Our sight grows dim, our limbs unsteady, our minds forgetful. Our parents, our siblings, and even our children die. Disease and injury invade and insult our bodies, take up residence and wage their wars of attrition. And no matter how fiercely we rage against the dying of the light, we all decline, decay, and dwindle.

And perhaps because we live in the shadow of this fear and impotence we often rail against our powerlessness by struggling to dominate, oppress, and marginalize other bodies. We try to escape our mortality and frailty by climbing on the backs of other bodies, by drawing lines between ourselves and the bodies of those who are our siblings, cousins, and neighbors. We flee from our own bodiliness by proclaiming that we are not like these other bodies, that we are different somehow from the sick and frail, from the bruised and broken, from the weak and lowly. And so we have built pyramids of bodies and scrambled to be the ones on top. We have taken out our rage about being mortal by beating and bruising the flesh of others. We have, as Shylock complains so bitterly, treated them like nobodies.

And so the very bodies that tie us to one another have become the markers of division and alienation. The uniqueness of our human flesh has become an excuse to abuse and pollute the body of nature. We have separated ourselves out from all the other bodies of creation and sought to dominate and/or consume the vast array of living organisms that are our hosts and kin. We have fled from our own bodiliness by turning the body of creation into a soulless machine that provides us with resources and disposes of our waste. And we have left carnage and death in our wake.

Within the human community we have drawn lines of demarcation based on real, imagined, or imposed differences between our bodies and the bodies of others, and we have all too often divided our communities into bodies that we care for and those we abandon or oppress. We have despised and punished other bodies because of their gender, their height, their weight—and the shade of their skin, the shape of their face, and the angle of their eyes. The body of humanity has been scarred by sexism, racism, and a plague of prejudices; and the bodies of women and countless minorities or oppressed peoples have been disfigured by these bigotries. We have shunned and shackled bodies that felt different sexual passions, ate different foods, spoke different languages, or dressed themselves in different garbs. We have discarded or destroyed sick or stunted bodies that did not live up to our ideal—diseased or disfigured bodies that reminded us of our own impotence, frailty, or mortality. We have classed whole communities of persons as nobodies because their bodies were like ours in every way but one. And we have separated ourselves into enclaves and ghettos where some bodies receive lavish care and others are disfigured by the ravages of hunger, poverty, violence, and despair. All too often being somebody has meant being a nobody in somebody else's eyes.

Taking Bodies Seriously

And how has Christianity understood what it means to be a somebody? In spite of some significant ambivalence about bodies, Christianity has recognized persons as somebodies and taken our bodies and the body of creation seriously. Our faith in creation and the sacramentality of the universe, as well as the incarnation and the resurrection, affirm that we are our bodies and that all the bodies of the cosmos are good, even holy.

As we read in the first chapter of Genesis, all of the bodies and body of creation have been made and blessed by God, and all of them are good, indeed *very* good. "God saw everything that he had made, and indeed, it was very good" (1:31). Our own human flesh, Scripture reports, has been formed by the hand of God, animated by the breath of God, and fashioned in the image and likeness of God. Genesis also tells us of God's care for all the bodies of creation, providing food and sustenance for every living creature (1:28-30) and placing humans in the garden to tend and look after the bodies of all our co-creatures (2:15). And in Matthew 6:26-30 we are reminded of how God continues to attend to even the smallest and least significant of our bodies, feeding the birds of the sky and clothing the grass in the fields.

All of these bodies, great and small, are also sacraments of God, and indeed the whole body of creation in all of its wondrous richness, complexity, and harmony is God's sacrament. This sacramentality refers to the way creation bodies forth and reveals the graciousness of God.[3] As Gerard Manley Hopkins notes, "the world is charged with the grandeur of God," and from every pebble, person, and planet this grandeur and grace bubbles up and spills over, "like shining from shook foil . . . like the ooze of oil."[4] In Wisdom 13:3-5 we read that God's glory and wisdom shine forth in her creation, and in Daniel 3:74-81 all of creation is urged to sing praises to their creator. According to Scripture and Christian theology the bodies and body of creation are thick with the scent of God's holiness, with the generosity and compassion of our creator. Simply by being themselves they reveal God's grace and so each of them, individually and collectively, is intrinsically good and sacred, even if *we* can find no use for one or the other of them. For in a very real sense all of them are the word of God made flesh and crying out our maker's praise.[5]

Still, even creation and the sacramentality of the world do not capture the full sanctity of our bodies or the seriousness with which Christian theology takes our embodiment. For in the mystery of the incarnation God has taken on our flesh and become a somebody in a radical, even scandalous way. In the person of Jesus, the one who formed and sustains all of the bodies of the universe and breathed life into the flesh of every living being, God has come among us as a somebody. The one who transcends all the boundaries and limits of our embodiment, whose fullness we cannot begin to grasp or name, has in some completely inexplicable manner *shuffled on* this mortal coil, *taken up* this frail and glorious flesh, and *become one* with us. And in taking on our embodiment and coming to dwell among us God has also somehow taken on the bodies of all persons and creatures—and the whole body of the cosmos. All flesh, all bodies have been touched and transformed by this encounter. As feminist and sacramental theologian Susan Ross notes, "because God has chosen to live with humanity in the flesh, all of human life has been transformed." Indeed, "Once God has elected to dwell among us, sharing our human condition, all of creation is profoundly affected."[6]

The resurrection of Christ has also taken up and transformed the bodies and body of creation. As the New Testament narratives make clear, Christ has been raised from the dead not as a phantom or ghost, but as a somebody, and in the risen Christ our fully-embodied humanity is liberated from sin and death. As Paul tells us, we are part of Christ's risen body, and by being baptized into Christ's death and resurrection we too, in all our embodied humanity, are transformed. And that transformation is not limited to human bodies. In Romans 8:18-25 we learn that all of the bodies and body of creation are liberated and transformed by Christ's death and resurrection.

Along with these doctrines, Scripture is full of evidence that God cares about bodies—and in particular about the bodies of those who are treated like nobodies. In Exodus 3:7-10 God is revealed as one who has heard the plaintive cries of the Hebrews and is moved to liberate them from their suffering and oppression. Over all the din and clamor of the Pharaoh's empire, God's ears have been pricked by the sound of slaves weeping over their backbreaking toil and murdered children. "I have observed the misery of my people who are in Egypt; I have heard their cry on account of their taskmasters. Indeed, I know their sufferings, and I have come down to deliver them from the Egyptians" (vv. 7-8).

And when this ragtag gathering of nobodies has been liberated from their taskmaster's rod and delivered into a land flowing with milk and honey, the God of the Hebrews reminds the Israelites again and again that their righteousness will not be measured by the number of their holocausts and sacrifices, but by their treatment of the burdened and broken bodies of other nobodies. As God reminds the Hebrews in Isaiah 58:6-7:

> Is not this the fast that I choose: to loose the bonds of injustice, to undo the thongs of the yoke, to let the oppressed go free, and to break every yoke? Is it not to share your bread with the hungry, and bring the homeless poor into your house; when you see the naked, to cover them, and not to hide yourself from your own kin?

Time and again the prophets remind the Hebrews of their ties and duties to the discarded bodies of widows, orphans, and aliens—and of God's passion for these nobodies.

Jesus too makes it clear that he is deeply concerned about what happens to our bodies, particularly to the overlooked or oppressed bodies of the poor and marginalized. In Luke 4:18-19 he announces that "The Spirit of the Lord . . . has anointed me to bring good news to the poor. He has sent me to proclaim release to the captives and recovery of sight to the blind, to let the oppressed go free." This concern for our suffering bodies also shows up in the various accounts of healing miracles and in parables that call us to love our neighbors by feeding their empty bellies, mopping their fevered brows, cleansing and binding their wounds, and clothing their nakedness. Identifying with these suffering nobodies, the Son of Man proclaims in Matthew 25:35-36, that "I was hungry and you gave me food, I was thirsty and you gave me something to drink, I was a stranger and you welcomed me, I was naked and you gave me clothing, I was sick and you took care of me, I was in prison and you visited me." Indeed, whenever you came to the aid of any of these bodies, however insignificant, you cared for me.

Those who followed after Jesus understood that to be a part of the Body of Christ meant to be in solidarity with the bodies of the suffering and dispossessed of the earth. So, as we have seen, the early Church described in Acts and elsewhere understood that to be Christ's body meant to feed bodies that were hungry, to offer hospitality and shelter to bodies that were poor and homeless, to nurse bodies that were sick, and to care for bodies that were dying. It also meant to recognize the full humanity and dignity of bodies that were being treated as nobodies and to reject divisions or preferences that honored some bodies but spurned others.

The importance of bodies was also seen in the call to practice the corporal works of mercy (feeding the hungry, sheltering the homeless, clothing the naked, visiting the sick and imprisoned, burying the dead, and giving alms to the poor) and in the rise of various church institutions and religious communities dedicated to the care of suffering bodies. In the fourth century Christians established hospitals for the sick and dying, and later expanded their ministries to provide for pilgrims, orphans, widows, and a wide range of the poor and disenfranchised. What's more, the Christian calendar is full of saints like Vincent de Paul and Elizabeth Ann Seton who spent their lives caring for the bodies of the sick and suffering.

And in the past century Catholic social thought and theologies of liberation have paid close attention to the cries of suffering bodies, especially those emanating from society's nobodies. At Vatican II, the Church declared that "the joys and hopes, the griefs and anxieties of the [people] of this age, especially those who are poor or in any way afflicted, these too are the joys and hopes, the griefs and anxieties of the followers of Christ."[7] And, as Sallie McFague notes, liberation theologies

> claim that the gospel of Jesus of Nazareth has a preferential option for the poor, the poor in body, those whose bodies and bodily needs are not included in the conventional hierarchy of value. These are bodies that are devalued, discarded, and destroyed; these are bodies that can claim no intrinsic value in themselves but are of worth only because they are useful to others.[8]

Still, although Christianity has affirmed the basic importance and goodness of bodies, as well as the fundamental integrity of persons as embodied spirits, Christian theology has also been marred by a certain ambivalence about bodies and has long been infected with a dualistic worldview that has denigrated the bodies and body of creation. As McFague argues in *The Body of God,* "Christianity is *par excellence* the religion of the incarnation and, in one sense, is about nothing but embodiment. . . . In another sense, . . . Christianity has denied, subjugated, and at times despised the body, especially female human bodies and bodies in the natural world."[9]

Susan Ross explores Christianity's ambivalence about bodies in a number of recent articles on sacramental theology and embodiment.[10] As Ross notes, Christianity rejected Gnostic assertions that bodies and matter were evil, but succumbed to a certain Neoplatonism, seeing the body as inferior and subject to the soul. As a result, early and medieval Christian theology developed a noticeable suspicion of the body.[11]

Augustine's teachings on sin and sexuality only deepened this suspicion. According to Augustine, human sinfulness was experienced primarily in concupiscence, a willful selfishness that he tended to associate with unruly bodily desires and pleasures, particularly those of a sexual nature. The result was that subsequent Christian thinkers stressed the ways our bodies had been tainted by sin, viewed bodily pleasures as particularly dangerous or evil, and argued that our flesh needed to be controlled and disciplined by our higher, spiritual, faculties.[12]

Christianity's suspicion and denigration of bodies and bodily pleasures (especially sex) was tied to a parallel denigration and suspicion of women. As Ross points out, Christian thinkers like Aquinas associated women more closely with bodies and sexuality, and "women's identification with the body has led elements in the tradition to see women as evil, or at least as potentially more evil than men."[13] Women were judged to be more bodily, more sexual, more passive, and at least potentially more sinful than men, having supposedly seduced or manipulated the first male into committing sin. This overidentification of women with bodies meant that they were seen as less spiritual, less intellectual, and less moral than their male counterparts, all of which was offered as justification for the ongoing subjugation and oppression of women and their bodies. Like our bodies, women were seen as passive, inferior, and potentially dangerous, needing the governance and discipline provided by men. This suspicion and hostility to the bodies of women extended to our sacramental life, where the bodies of women were systematically excluded from roles of ministry and leadership in the sanctuary, and where the Church has taught that while all of us belong to and make up the Body of Christ, only male bodies are truly fit sacraments of Christ's presence in the Eucharist.[14]

The Eucharist and the Church

In spite of Christianity's ambivalence about bodies, however, we speak about the Eucharist and the Church as the Body of Christ. And in doing so we express our faith that the risen Christ is truly present both in the breaking of the bread and in the community of disciples gathered around the table of the Eucharist. Even more, calling the Eucharist and the Church the Body of Christ affirms God and Christ's radical communion with our bodies and our own solidarity with the bodies of our neighbors. In this section, then, we will look at what it means to speak about the Eucharist and the Church as the Body of Christ and what the moral implications are of eating and being part of this body.

We have already seen that the early disciples came to recognize and remember the risen Christ in the breaking of the bread and that the Eucharist was experienced as a real encounter with the mystery and person of Jesus Christ. In the centuries that followed the eucharistic faith of the Church was expressed in the firm belief that Christ is really and sacramentally present in the Eucharist in the form of bread and wine. In the course of the eucharistic prayer the bread and wine are transformed into Christ's Body and Blood and those of us who share in this meal are nurtured by and joined to this body. Indeed, in the Eucharist we celebrate our identity and vocation as the Body of Christ. We are knitted into this body and commissioned to be this body to and for the world.

Still, within the Eucharist, Christ is not embodied in the bread and wine alone, but bodies forth in the whole eucharistic celebration, in our being gathered together to hear God's word and offer praise and thanksgiving, and in our being sent forth to proclaim and practice the Good News. Indeed, the Church teaches that the risen Christ is truly present to us in the community of believers assembled around the table, the Word of God proclaimed in the biblical readings, the minister who presides in Christ's name, and the eucharistic food being blessed and shared.[15]

And there is a particularly intimate and dynamic relationship between the presence of Christ in the Eucharist and the presence of Christ in the Church. For it is the Church as Body of Christ that gathers and celebrates the Eucharist, and the Eucharist as Body of Christ that nurtures and transforms the Church into Christ's body. As the theologian Peter Fink notes, when the minister proclaims "the Body of Christ" to those approaching the table,

> this is a deliberately multivalent statement meaning at one and the same time the bread, the eating of the bread, and what we, the

church, become in the eating. This simple acclamation capsulizes
. . . (our prayer) that the food become the body and blood of
Christ, and that we who eat and drink become one body and one
spirit in Christ.[16]

And to this we say *"Amen."* Eugene LaVerdiere makes a similar point
when he argues that the

> liturgical proclamation, "This is my body, which will be given for
> you," recalls the words of Christ offering himself, and speaks the
> words of the Church associating itself with Christ's offering and
> making his offering present sacramentally. The body given is
> that of Christ. It is also that of the church, the sacrament of the
> Body of Christ.[17]

The link associating the Eucharist and the Church with the Body
of Christ and with one another is an ancient one. In the early Church,
as LaVerdiere points out,

> The Lord's Supper and the words, 'This is my body' . . . referred
> to the person or self of Christ and to their own personal self as a
> community in Christ. . . . In the Eucharist, Christians offered
> themselves and their whole life with, in and through Christ, and
> continued Christ's life and mission to all peoples.[18]

As we saw earlier, Paul often speaks about the Church as the Body
of Christ, and indeed describes this body as a communion *(koinonia)*
formed and sustained by sharing in the one bread of the Eucharist.
Paul's first encounter with the risen Christ comes on the road to
Damascus, where he is headed to persecute Christians (Acts 9:3-5). A
great light flashes from the sky and Paul falls to the ground, hearing
this question, "Saul, Saul, why do you persecute me?" Asking who it
is that speaks, Paul is told "I am Jesus, whom you are persecuting." By
persecuting the members of the Church, the future apostle to the
Gentiles learns, Paul has been attacking the Body of Christ.[19]

And so Paul instructs his listeners that all the baptized have died
with Christ and been joined to the risen body *(soma)* and person of the
resurrected Christ. "Do you not know that your bodies are members
of Christ?" Paul asks in First Corinthians 6:15. Later in the same letter
he notes that "just as the body is one and has many members, and all
the members of the body, though many, are one body, so it is with

Christ. For in the one Spirit we were all baptized into one body—Jews or Greeks, slaves or free—and we were all made to drink of one Spirit" (12:12-13).

In Romans 12:4-5, also, the apostle writes, "For as in one body we have many members, and not all the members have the same function, so we, who are many, are one body in Christ, and individually we are members one of another."

For Paul there is an intimate connection between the Church as Body of Christ and the Eucharist, since the unity of the body is confirmed by the sharing of all disciples in the one table of the Lord. As he writes in First Corinthians 10:16-17, "The cup of blessing that we bless, is it not a sharing in the blood of Christ? The bread that we break, is it not a sharing in the body of Christ? Because there is one bread, we who are many are one body, for we all partake of the one bread."

By the same token, any divisions or injustices tearing at the fabric of the Church will also undermine the celebration of the Eucharist. When wealthy members of the church in Corinth divide and dishonor the Body of Christ by failing to break bread with their poorer neighbors, Paul accuses them of failing to "discern the body" and concludes that the very meal they eat condemns them. For they are neither sharing nor being the Body of Christ. "Examine yourselves, and only then eat of the bread and drink of the cup. For all who eat and drink *without discerning the body,* eat and drink judgment against themselves" (emphasis added; 1 Cor 11:28-29).

In the twentieth century, the American Benedictine monk, liturgist, and social activist Virgil Michel took up this Pauline understanding of the Church as the Body of Christ and the Eucharist as the central sacrament of that communion. Like Paul, Michel was concerned that too few Christians "recognized the body" they shared in the Eucharist or belonged to in the Church. In an age shaped by individualism and materialism most believers saw the Eucharist as a private encounter with Christ and thought of their membership in the Church as a spiritual, otherworldly communion. Describing the Church as the mystical Body of Christ, Michel argued that the members of the Church were tied not only to the risen Christ but also to all the other members of this body. Being a member of the Church meant being in real, not merely spiritual, solidarity and communion with other members of Christ—and living out that solidarity in our public, political, economic, and social lives. Indeed, the Church as the mystical Body of

Christ should be a leaven for this solidarity in the larger world, helping to overcome the selfish isolation of individualism and the social divisions created by greed, prejudice, and injustice by standing with the victims of poverty, discrimination, and oppression. In light of this, Michel called for liturgical reforms that would help Christians to recognize the Body of Christ in the Eucharist and the Church, that would help us see and experience our real and vibrant communion with each other and our vocation to be the Body of Christ for the world.[20] Through more active and conscious participation in the breaking of the bread, Christians would come to see their membership in the Body of Christ and practice that membership in the world around them.

The lessons from both Paul and Virgil Michel are that there are moral implications of our sharing in and being part of the Body of Christ. Taking part in the Eucharist and being members of the Church tie us to other members of Christ's body and to all the other bodies and body of creation. As the priest and activist Paul Hanly Furfey wrote over six decades ago:

> How great a mystery is the Communion [Eucharist]! We receive our Divine Lover, His sacred Body, His precious Blood, His very Soul and Divinity, but together with Him we are brought into communion with all humanity. For Christ the Head is inseparable from His members. The parts of a living body must be in active union with one another; otherwise it would not be a living body. . . . The Mass [Eucharist] outlaws economic injustice and race prejudice and war. It leads us to see these social problems in the true light, as foolish sins against the Mystical Body. Moreover the Mass, as an inexhaustible source of grace gives us the strength and courage to overcome our own selfishness and practice heroic charity.[21]

The implications, then, of discerning the body, of sharing in and being a member of the Body of Christ are twofold. To take part in the Eucharist and belong to the Church means that we are being summoned to be in solidarity with all the bodies and body of creation, particularly the wounded and broken bodies of the poor, oppressed, and marginalized. It also means that we are called to bodily resist and overcome every sort of division and alienation that wounds and scars the Body of Christ by dishonoring or abandoning some of its members, by treating them as nobodies. Paraphrasing Matthew 5:23-24, we cannot come to the table where the body is gathered or shared unless we are willing to recognize and honor all the bodies invited to this communion.

In the incarnation God not only took on human flesh, but reached out in a particular way to the bodies of the poor and outcast. As R. Kevin Seasoltz notes, "One of the most crucial and yet most disturbing aspects of the incarnation is that Jesus identified above all with the poor; he designated them as the privileged heirs of his kingdom; he took their side and defended them against their oppressors."[22] Sallie McFague makes a similar point, noting that

> the story of Jesus suggests that the shape of God's body includes all, especially the needy and outcast. . . . The distinctive characteristic of Christian embodiment is its focus on oppressed, vulnerable, suffering bodies, those who are in pain due to the indifference or greed of the more powerful.[23]

Moreover, the Church, as what John Haughey has called the "social flesh" of Christ, must stand in solidarity with the wounded and broken bodies of all the victims of poverty, violence, and injustice. Those of us who have taken on the flesh of Christ in baptism are called to tend and care for the bodies of the sick and suffering, to accompany the bodies of the abandoned, neglected, and dying. And this care for the suffering bodies of our neighbors must also extend to the bodies of all our fellow creatures and to the often abused and disfigured body of creation. As the Body of Christ the Church must continue the Incarnation's preferential option for all the world's nobodies.

This solidarity with the suffering bodies of our neighbors and co-creatures, however, extends beyond offering care. Those of us who share in the Eucharist and belong to the Church are called to actively resist the structures and systems of injustice and oppression that burden and break the bodies of the poor. We are called to place our bodies in the paths of these powers, to stand with the victims and to raise up our voices in their defense.

At the same time, sharing in and belonging to the Body of Christ also means that we must work to overcome and dismantle every division and privilege that mars the communion of the Eucharist, the Church or the human community.[24] As the author of Galatians 3:27-28 writes, "As many of you as were baptized into Christ have clothed yourselves with Christ. There is no longer Jew or Greek, there is no longer slave or free, there is no longer male and female; for all of you are one in Christ Jesus" Discerning the body means unmasking and removing every structure and practice that dishonors the body by treating some bodies as if they were nobodies. In our present world there are three particularly striking ways in which we are called to be the Body of Christ: by standing with the bodies of the poor, by honoring the bodies of women, and by recognizing our kinship with the bodies and body of creation.

Solidarity with the Bodies of the Poor

Because we are bodies, we are needy. We need food and drink, clothing and shelter, room to move about, and the comforting company of other bodies. Without these we die, which leads us to a second point. Because we are bodies we are also frail, vulnerable, and mortal. We get sick and injured, grow tired and old, fall ill and die. For large chunks of our lives many of us manage to live without noticing our neediness and frailty, and we have a name for all those bodies that cannot mask their hunger or mortality, who remind us of the downside of our embodiment—the poor.

The poor are all the somebodies in our midst who cannot meet their basic needs, who cannot find enough food and drink, clothing and shelter, or comfort from other bodies. They are the bodies who cannot protect themselves or their children from hunger and thirst, cold and danger. They are the bodies being devoured and disfigured by want, and the constant reminder of the neediness of our own flesh. The poor are also all the somebodies overwhelmed by their frailty. They are the unprotected bodies invaded by disease and overrun by sickness, the bodies scarred and sapped by their encroaching mortality. And the cries of their bodies are a plaintive call for compassion and care.

Still, the poor are not merely those bodies overwhelmed by need and frailty, nor simply a reminder of our own hunger and mortality. They are also, even largely, the victims of injustice, oppression, and marginalization—and the cries of their suffering bodies are the complaints and accusations of those being crushed, abused, or abandoned by structures and communities that treat them as nobodies. Colonialism, racism, sexism, militarism, and consumerism have scarred and broken the suffering bodies of countless poor, and the cries of all these nobodies are also the groans of a larger body sick with injustice and violence. More than a summons to compassion, these cries are a trumpet call to reform, a command to heal our diseased political, economic, and cultural bodies by learning to honor, care for, and stand with all the bodies of the abandoned, oppressed, and disappeared.

To share in and be a part of the Body of Christ, then, means hearing the cries of the bodies of the poor and coming to their aid. It means recognizing these laments as coming from suffering and sacred bodies that are one in flesh with us, that are indeed the flesh of the risen Christ. And it means hearing these cries as the voice of Christ calling us to care for and stand with all these so-called nobodies in their struggle for survival, liberation, and justice. In Exodus (3:7-10) God awakens Moses to the cries of the suffering bodies of the Hebrews and summons him to liberate them from the forces of injustice and oppression. And in Deuteronomy (10:18), Jeremiah (22:3-4), and Isaiah (58:6-7) YHWH commands the Hebrews to hear the lament of widows, orphans, and aliens, to recognize their solidarity with these bodies so overwhelmed by want and injustice, and to reform their communities in ways that honor and make room for these bodies. In his miracles and ministry Jesus responds to the cries of all sorts of suffering bodies—the blind and the lame, the possessed and the leprous, the epileptic and the dying—and Matthew (25:31-46) has the Son of Man taking sides with every sort of body overwhelmed by want and frailty.

The members of the church of Acts (2:42-47 and 4:32-37) saw a deep connection between their being a communion formed by the breaking of the bread and their duty to respond to the wounded Body of Christ—to feed the hungry, clothe the naked, and shelter the homeless. "There was not a needy person among them, for as many as owned lands or houses sold them and brought the proceeds of what was sold. They laid it at the apostles' feet, and it was distributed to each as any had need" (4:34-35). They also understood that being the Body of Christ meant that they must resist every bias and division that could sunder this body by privileging some bodies and ignoring others. And so reports of discrimination against Greek-speaking widows was seen as a threat to the very fabric of the Church.

As we saw earlier, this link between being the Body of Christ and recognizing and standing with the wounded Body of Christ in the poor led early Christians to take up a collection for the poor at their Eucharist and then to found all sorts of institutions and communities dedicated to caring for the suffering bodies of the poor.[25] Indeed, in the fourth century John Chrysostom argued that although the eucharistic table was sacred "because it receives the Body of Christ," the body of the poor person is sacred "it is the Body of Christ."[26] In the seventeenth century Vincent de Paul advised his colleagues that any one who left the Eucharist to attend to the needs of a poor person at the door was "leaving Christ for Christ." And in the twentieth century Christians like Dorothy Day reaffirmed that our common membership in the Body of Christ impelled us to care for and stand with the suffering bodies of all the world's poor and outcasts. "The mystery of the poor is this: that they are Jesus and what you do for them you do for Him."[27] Again and again Christians have understood that sharing in and being part of the Body of Christ obliges us to recognize Christ in the suffering bodies of the poor and to minister to these sacred bodies as we would to Christ's own. For sharing in and being part of the Body of Christ means making a preferential option for the bodies of the poor.

Making this preferential option for the bodies of the poor makes demands on our bodies as well. Caring for and siding with the wounded flesh of Christ requires that we become—both individually and corporately—different kinds of bodies. Down through the centuries Christians who sought to live out their vocation as members of the Body of Christ soon discovered that tending to and standing with the bodies of the poor required that their own bodies undergo a transformation. To share their goods and life with the poor they would need to overcome their own bodily attachments to possessions and comfort—and to surrender many of the goods and privileges that separated them from the wounded Body of Christ. To tend and care lovingly for bodies wracked and disfigured by poverty and injustice, they would need to learn to recognize the face of Christ in even the most wounded human flesh, and to honor and revere that flesh in spite of any distaste or fear. And in order to stand with the poor against all the forces of injustice and violence they would need to forge their bodies into a corps of martyrs giving testimony to the love of Christ.

And so we pray in the Eucharist not only that the bread and wine be transformed into the Body and Blood of Christ, but also that those of us gathered around the table will undergo a change. We pray that in the Eucharist our bodies may be transformed into the sorts of bodies that see, judge, and act differently. Our prayer is that this communion will forge us into bodies and a body that recognize the risen Christ in the faces and bodies of the poor, and that remember Christ by re-membering ourselves to the wounded flesh of the poor. And we pray that the body of believers gathered to celebrate the Eucharist will be transformed into a body whose scars of division, oppression, and bias are overcome by the love of Christ, and whose communion is a sacrament and leaven of peace and justice for the world.

The transformation of our bodies that we pray for in the Eucharist begins with the change from an acquisitive to a generous heart. We pray that we might be freed of the attachments to wealth and comfort that separate us from the bodies of the poor. In Luke's parable of the rich man and the beggar Lazarus (16:19-31) it is greed that keeps the wealthy man from noticing the suffering body of the poor man at his gate. And when Jesus encounters a rich young man who cannot let go of his wealth, we are told that "it is easier for a camel to go through the eye of a needle than for someone who is rich to enter the kingdom of God" (Matt 19:24).

For two millennia Christians have understood that an attachment to wealth blinds us to the needs of the poor, and that caring for the bodies of the poor demanded embracing a spirit of voluntary poverty or simplicity. The church of Acts, the early monastic communities that practiced hospitality to the poor, the legions of religious orders whose members have run hospitals, orphanages, foundling homes, shelters, and soup kitchens—and the countless other Christians who practice these and other corporal works of mercy—have all known that hearing the cries of the poor and tending to the wounded flesh of Christ means overcoming our own addictive attachments to possessions and sharing one's goods with those in need.[28]

Today, as we are increasingly aware that poverty is all too often the fruit of greed and injustice, and when the divide between the world's rich and poor continues to increase, there is an even greater need for us to pray for bodies liberated from the attachments that divide us from our neighbors. As we saw earlier, we live in a consumerist society that schools our bodies to desire and possess more and more, even if this escalating appetite threatens the survival of billions. From earliest childhood we are bombarded with messages that seek to "brand" and shape us into bodies that are never satisfied and always hungry, and this formation is driving our hearts and minds and bodies further and further from the suffering bodies of the poor and is threatening the very fabric of community.[29] In the Eucharist we pray that our bodies and the body of our community may be transformed, that we may be bodies liberated from the shackles of escalating, addictive, and isolating attachments—that we may be bodies capable of hearing and attending to the cries of the poor, of recognizing and re-membering ourselves to the wounded Body of Christ.

We also pray that our bodies may be changed in ways that will enable us to stand with the bodies of the poor, to join them in resisting all the forces of injustice that oppress and marginalize them, and to face with them the reactive violence that is unleashed whenever the weak and powerless stand up for their rights. In the Eucharist we pray to be changed into bodies that hear the cries of the tortured, the disappeared, the persecuted, the marginalized, the abused, the oppressed, and the violated. We pray to be transformed into bodies that are willing to go and stand with these nobodies, to take up their burdens and walk around inside their skin, to take on their flesh and dwell among them. And we pray to be forged into the sorts of bodies that will become a living phalanx standing against the injustice and violence being unleashed against the suffering bodies of the poor.

As M. Therese Lysaught and Maureen Tilley note, the early Church resisted persecution and torture by training bodies to become martyrs.[30] In and through the Eucharist the Church forged itself into a body that testified to Christ in the face of persecution and that formed believers into embodied witnesses to that faith—witnesses who could not be turned into nobodies by torture or death. In a similar fashion the civil rights workers of the 1950s and 1960s underwent a formation process in which they trained their own bodies in the practice of nonviolent resistance and in doing so created a living corps of witnesses from which the public eye could not turn away. The bodies of these young women and men who would not sit or stand as they were told; who would not be neither silenced, broken, or hosed down; and who would not be provoked into retaliatory violence or hatred became a leaven in the community that changed the face of history.

In the Eucharist we pray to be changed into such bodies. We pray to be transformed into bodies like Dorothy Day and Oscar Romero, bodies ready to go and stand with the bodies of the poor. We pray for the courage and compassion to be changed into a body that sides with the oppressed. And we pray to become the sorts of bodies that can turn our cheek and stand against the face of violence without being formed in its image and likeness. We pray to be changed into the Body of Christ.

Solidarity with the Bodies of Women

Galatians 3:28 tells us that "There is no longer . . . male and female; for all of you are one in Christ Jesus." Our union in the one flesh of the risen Christ is incompatible with any segregation based on gender, with any discrimination against the bodies of women. During his life Jesus repeatedly challenged patriarchal and sexist practices and structures that excluded or oppressed women, including women among his close friends, table companions, and disciples.[31] And in the community that recognized and remembered Christ in the breaking of the bread, women were acknowledged as the first witnesses to the resurrection and served as prophets, missionaries, deacons, apostles, and the leaders of local churches.[32]

Unfortunately, the Body of Christ that gathered around the eucharistic table was soon wounded by sexism and patriarchy, and in the centuries that followed the Church generally envisioned and treated the bodies of women as inferior and subject to the bodies of men.[33] Women were portrayed as intellectually, spiritually, and morally inferior to men, and not infrequently as the source of (usually carnal) temptation. The privilege and power of male bodies went unchallenged by Church teachings that called women to subservience and obedience, excluded them from leadership in their homes or church, and tended to limit their identity as persons or disciples to their (usually misunderstood) reproductive role.[34] Augustine wrote that women lacked reason and only possessed the image of God through their connection with men. Aquinas argued that women were misbegotten males, and saw them as less rational, spiritual, and perfect than males. And Pope Pius XI denied the notion that husbands and wives were equals.[35]

Women have been described as more bodily, sensual, sexual, and sinful than men, and this bias has served to justify the marginalization and exclusion of women's bodies. In our liturgies women's bodies have not been deemed worthy to stand in for or near the sacred. Only male language and images were judged appropriate for speaking about and to God, and only male bodies have been viewed as capable of fully representing Christ at the altar. Even though, as Christine Gudorf points out, most of our sacraments celebrate the sorts of nurturing activities and routines normally carried out by women, only men have been allowed to perform these rituals in the sanctuary.[36] Women, who make up more than half of the Body of Christ, can be the *bride* of Christ, but cannot represent the head of the body, cannot be an *alter Christus*. Indeed, they have not only been excluded from the priesthood but also removed almost completely from the sanctuary. As Teresa Berger notes, by "the Middle Ages women were on the whole virtually excluded from . . . the sanctuary," and even today "women are largely invisible in liturgical celebrations."[37]

The bodies of women have also been marginalized in the workplace and corridors of political power. Women are generally the preferred employees in sweatshops because they can be paid less and are more easily exploited.[38] Putting in two-third's of the world's work hours, they earn one-tenth of the world's income, in no small part because they do the vast majority of its unpaid and underpaid domestic labor, and because they make up the bulk of bodies in the low-paying "service" sector.[39] Moreover, whenever the "dirty" work of caring for and cleaning up behind the bodies of our infants, infirm, or aged needs to be done, whether in our homes, hospitals, hospices, or hotels, it is invariably a burden that is placed on the backs of women.[40] Here in the U.S. the labor of a woman's body continues to earn less than three-quarters as much as a man's, while women entering the workforce are expected to face the twin hurdles of securing adequate childcare and taking on a second shift of domestic labor at the end of their "official" workday. And a glass ceiling continues to make it as tough for many women to enter executive boardrooms as it would be for a camel to sew. Meanwhile, women's bodies make up less than one-seventh of the senators and representatives serving in the U.S. Congress, and no woman has yet been elected to the presidency or vice-presidency.[41]

The belief that women are morally, intellectually, and spiritually inferior to men has also justified a global plague of abuse against the bodies of women. A Vatican statement on *The Roots of Domestic Violence* reports that there is "no doubt that violence against women has as its root cause a diffuse, mostly unexpressed conviction that women are not equal to men and that therefore it is normal for a man to subject women to his own will or to have them serve his pleasure."[42] Unfortunately, these sexist and patriarchal beliefs have found ample support and expression in the teachings and practices of most Christian Churches.[43] As the U.S. Catholic bishops have acknowledged, "we are called to recognize that sexist attitudes have also colored Church teaching and practice over the centuries and still in our day."[44]

Violence against the bodies of women is massive and pervasive. Christine Gudorf writes that "there is little doubt that most women live in fear, to greater or lesser degrees, of male anger and aggression."[45] And J. Milburn Thompson reports that

> In nearly every country, across all classes, women are beaten by their husbands and fathers, assaulted and raped by relatives, acquaintances, and strangers, and harassed and intimidated on the street, in school, and at work. . . . This sexual violence is not random; it is aimed at women as women, and meant to frighten and control them. It amounts to 'sexual terrorism,' a system perpetuated by men for the domination of women.[46]

According to the U.S. Catholic bishops, "domestic violence is the most common form of violence in our society and the least-reported crime."[47] Every year 1,500 women in the U.S. are killed by their current or former boyfriends or spouses, while another 3 to 4 million are battered by such men. More than 50% of women in this country are battered at some point in their lives. More than one-third are assaulted repeatedly each year. Assaults by intimate partners result in more injuries that require medical treatment than rape, auto accidents, and muggings combined. "In the U.S. nine out of ten women murdered are killed by men known to them; four out of five are murdered at home."[48]

Nor is this the only abuse of women's bodies. Every year two million girls—some as young as four years old—join the over 100 million women worldwide who have been forced to undergo female genital mutilation, usually without anesthesia.[49] Women of every age are more likely than men to experience hunger and be trapped in poverty, and vastly more likely to be left to raise their children without aid. At the same time numerous studies indicate that the bodies of women are less likely to receive adequate medical care.

The bodies of women are also abused by a male gaze that wanders between voyeurism and pornography and is not always content merely to look. Margaret Miles describes the enduring obsession of our popular media with the bodies of women: "The young female body has been adopted by North American consumer society as a vehicle for selling everything from cars to cigarettes. . . . Contemporary images of half-clothed Eves, Judiths and Susannas appear regularly in newspapers and magazines, on television, and in films." The effect of this obsession is to "lock in place a public gaze that fixes women's bodies as objects of voyeurism: unclothed or partially unclothed, fetishized, often posed in unbalanced postures."[50]

One result of this obsessive gaze has been to reduce the bodies of women, offering young women and girls progressively smaller and thinner versions of themselves, pressuring and urging them to become thinner and thinner. As Miles notes, "thirty years ago the average model in North American advertising weighed 8% less than the average woman; five years ago, the average model weighed 23% less than the average woman."[51] We shouldn't be surprised then, when we read that

> one third of 12- to 13-year-old girls are actively trying to lose weight by dieting, vomiting, using laxatives or taking diet pills; [that] the single largest group of high school students considering or attempting suicide are girls who think they're overweight, [that] half of all American women are dieting at any one time, or that over 90 percent of the people in this country suffering from eating disorders are young women.[52]

The male gaze of the media is also obsessed with the youthfulness of the female body and looks scornfully (or not at all) at the bodies of women over forty. Male actors continue to perform as romantic leads well into their late sixties and early seventies, but female media icons begin to fade from the screen in their mid thirties and early forties. And the same age discrimination marginalizes the bodies and faces of female news anchors and talk show hosts. Whenever the male glance of the media turns to women's bodies it wants only to see youth. No wonder, then, that so many middle-aged (and younger) women seek out plastic surgeons to keep them looking younger. In 1998 certified plastic surgeons in the U.S. performed over one million cosmetic procedures (liposuction, eye surgery, tummy tucks, facelifts), and fewer than one-tenth of these operations were on males.[53]

And when that gaze seeks to undress and dominate the bodies of women in pornography it inflicts yet another set of harms. Pornography, which is primarily a male gaze at female (and juvenile) bodies, trivializes and objectifies women, reducing them to entertainments and playthings meant to serve men's pleasure. It also encourages the domination and control of women's bodies, offering a view of women as passive sexual servants prepared to do whatever men ask of them, or as evil dominatrixes who need to overcome and punish. And all too often pornography degrades women by portraying them as willing or unwilling victims of sexual and physical violence, no doubt encouraging this behavior in a significant number of men and boys.[54]

The gaze that reduces women's bodies to sexual objects is also behind a burgeoning international sex tourism industry that has trapped millions upon millions of impoverished women and children in lives of degradation, violence, and disease beyond most of our worst nightmares. In Asia, Latin America, and Eastern Europe millions of poor women have been forced or manipulated into laboring as prostitutes for foreign tourists and visiting military personnel. Living in squalid conditions and often servicing as many as fifteen clients per evening, these women are being thrown onto the frontlines of a spreading epidemic of AIDS and other sexually transmitted diseases.[55]

Sharing in and being part of the Body of Christ obliges us to recognize and honor the full equality, dignity, and sanctity of the bodies of women. It means learning to imagine the bodies of women as made in the image and likeness of God (not men) and seeing them as fully adequate sacraments and symbols of the body and person of Christ. It means refashioning our liturgies to make room for feminist language, symbols, and rituals—and reshaping our sanctuaries and naves to make room for the bodies of women. It means resisting and dismantling every sexist and patriarchal ideology, structure, and practice protecting the privilege and power of men and wounding the Body of Christ. It means standing with all the victims of domestic and sexual violence and redistributing the burdens that have fallen disproportionately on the backs of women. It means praying to become the sort of body where there is neither male nor female.

Kinship with the Bodies and Body of Creation

As we saw earlier, the mystery of creation affirms the fundamental goodness and sanctity of all the bodies and the body of the universe. The first chapter of Genesis is a hymn to the wonder of creation, a sonnet in which we read that God has fashioned and blessed each and every body in the cosmos, provided for their nurturing and sustenance, and then stepped back and marveled at the goodness of her handiwork, for "it was very good" (1:31). For Christianity the bodies and body of nature are thick with the graciousness and glory of God. Each in their individual and unique splendor and all of them together in their symphonic harmony sing the praises of the one who fashioned and loves them.

The sanctity and goodness of all the bodies and body of creation has been driven home even further for Christians by God's nearly scandalous embracing of our embodiment in the incarnation. For in taking on our flesh and dwelling among us God has lavished on our bodies and the body of creation a love and sanctity that defies the imagination and settles into the marrow of our bones, the links of our DNA, and the quarks of our atoms.

Still, Christianity has often failed to honor the sanctity of creation, and Christian societies have all too often treated the bodies and body of nature with disregard and disdain. In the European colonization of the New World and the Industrial and Postindustrial Revolutions, Christian nations and peoples have ravaged and pillaged entire ecosystems and brought the planet to the precipice of ecological disaster. Massive forests have been cut down and plowed under, stripping the earth bare of any protection and destroying the habitats of countless species. Beasts both great and small have been hunted and fished into extinction, while our soil, water, and air have been poisoned and polluted by our tireless and escalating consumption. For most of the Christian era, particularly for the last five centuries, we have treated nature as a foe to be vanquished and subjugated—or a storehouse to be pillaged. And, as Christian ethicist James Nash has pointed out, "Christianity does bear part of the burden of guilt for our ecological crisis."[56]

A large part of Christianity's failure to honor and protect the bodies—and body—of creation flows from a distorted emphasis on the command in Genesis 1:28 to "fill the earth and subdue it; and have dominion over the fish of the sea and over the birds of the air and over every living thing that moves upon the earth." In "The Historical Roots of Our Ecological Crisis," cultural historian Lynn White argues that the Judeo-Christian tradition—with its biblical mandate to subdue and have dominion over the earth and all its creatures—is largely to blame for the current ecological crisis.[57] As White sees it, Christianity's use of "dominion" language has been used to justify all sorts of environmentally irresponsible and reckless attitudes, and behavior by the human community.

According to feminist theologian Elizabeth Johnson, the problem is that "dominion" language has been used to support a "kingship" model of humanity's relationship to the rest of creation. This model,

> sees humanity separated from the earth and placed in a position of absolute dominion over all other creatures who are made for us. In this view, the creatures of the world are ranked . . . with greater value being assigned to those up on the great chain of being. . . . In the progression from the pebble to the peach to the poodle to the person, with women somewhere between the latter two, the higher order of creatures has the right to use and control the lower. . . . This is the patriarchal pyramid again, resulting in a top-down domination of nature by man.[58]

This domination of the bodies and body of creation has been further abetted by the rise of a mechanistic view of nature. As Carolyn Merchant and Larry Rasmussen point out, the industrial age brought about a new worldview, no longer envisioning the earth as a life-giving and nurturing mother, with whom humans must live in harmony, but as a problem to be solved or an object to be controlled, dominated, and manipulated. As an example of this worldview, the philosopher Francis Bacon argued that nature should be "forced out of her natural state and squeezed and molded."[59] This objectification of nature and of the earth has fueled the current ecological crisis. For our problems with pollution, global warming, the depletion of rainforests, and other "natural resources," as well as the massive extinction of plant and animal species, all flow from a lack of respect for the bodies and body of creation.

Many Christian voices have sought to counteract "dominion" language and the "kingship" model by reminding us that humans are called to be stewards of creation. The U.S. Catholic bishops have called Christians to be "faithful stewards" of God's creation, and the Evangelical Lutheran Church in America has noted that this means that "we are called to care for the earth as God cares for the earth, . . . to serve and keep God's garden, the earth, . . . [and] to live according to God's wisdom in creation."[60] The biblical notion of stewardship reminds us of our duties to tend and care for the other bodies and body of creation, for in Genesis 2:15 humans are placed in the garden "to till it and keep it." At the same time, the notion of stewardship reminds us that any "dominion" or "lordship" that we exercise is to be carried out as *servants*. For as Christians we are always called to imitate the topsy-turvy dominion or lordship of Christ, who took the form of a servant (Phil 2:7) and washed the feet of his disciples (John 13:2-16).

This servant-lordship that we are to exercise as God's stewards also calls us to recognize the wounded Body of Christ in the ravaged bodies and body of creation, and to come to the aid of these bodies, resisting the forces that degrade, deplete, and destroy them—and groaning with them in the struggle for liberation. As Sallie McFague notes:

> The story of Jesus suggests that the shape of God's body includes all, especially the needy and outcast. While there are many distinctive features of the Christian notion of embodiment, in an ecological age when the development of our sensibility concerning the vulnerability and destruction of nonhuman creatures and the natural environment is critical, we ought to focus on one: the inclusion of the neglected oppressed—the planet itself and its many different creatures.[61]

Still, a number of Christian thinkers argue that stewardship does not go far enough, and they propose a model of "kinship" to describe humanity's relationship to all the co-creatures who make up the bodies and body of creation. According to Elizabeth Johnson, this kinship model "sees human beings and the earth with all its creatures intrinsically related as companions in a community of life. . . . [it] does not measure differences on a scale of higher or lower ontological dignity but appreciates them as integral elements in the robust thriving of a whole."[62] Johnson's notion of kinship does not imply that there are no "distinctions between human beings and other forms of life," only that the relationship of humanity to the rest of creation should be marked not by superiority, but interconnectedness and mutuality.

Perhaps no Christian has articulated this human kinship with creation as beautifully as Francis of Assisi in his famous "Canticle of Brother Sun," which proclaims that humans are sisters and brothers to all creation because we are all fashioned by the creative hand of God. In an essay on the Body of Christ, Bernard Lee offers an eloquent contemporary description of this kinship we are called to with the bodies and body of creation:

> We sisters and brothers of planet Earth must reconnect with the far reaches of the larger social system: all things are yours, and you are Christ's, and Christ is God's! [See 1 Cor 3:22-23.] The spirituality called for by a thorough-going ecology is not merely consistent with the Body of Christ but is implicit in it. Human history cannot continue to give nurture to Christ's Body unless we members of the Body treat our earth home far more benevolently than has been our wont. Our times are giving birth to a new word—*ecospirituality*. The terminology may or may not be passing, but the call to create a world that can support a Body is a call from the Body for the Body.[63]

Scripture confirms our kinship with the other bodies and body of the cosmos, pointing to our common origins and God's common concern for us. In Genesis 1:26-27 God creates humans as part and parcel of the larger work of creation, and in Genesis 2:7, 9, and 19 we read that humans are made of the same soil and clay that God used to create the plants and trees that cover the earth, the birds that fill the sky, and all the animals that roam the planet. Later, in Genesis 9:15, God makes a covenant with: "you [human beings] and every living creature of all flesh" and both Colossians 1:15-20 and Revelation 21:1-8 remind us that *all* of the bodies and body of creation share in the salvation of Christ.

Nor are these the only ways Scripture portrays humans as companions of the rest of creation. In Genesis 1:27 we learn that humans are made in the image of God as male and female. According to Michael and Kenneth Himes, this means that "God is relational," and that "to be the image of this God, the human being must be relational," not only with other humans but with all of creation itself.[64] In Genesis 1:31, it is the whole community of creation that God blesses as very good, a community into which humans come as co-creatures, kin, and companions. And in Genesis 2:18 God notes that "It is not good that the man should be alone," and God brings forth all sorts of animals as companions from the same soil as humans had been fashioned. Thus, even if the partnership between humans is different from the kinship we have with other creatures, Scripture teaches that humans come to the rest of creation as companions, and not merely as users or consumers.

Sharing in and being part of the Body of Christ calls us to acknowledge our fundamental kinship with the bodies and body of creation and to tend to and stand with the wounded Body of Christ, a body that includes not only impoverished and oppressed humans, but also the *anawim* (God's little ones) that make up the body of our co-creatures. In some very real sense the Eucharist challenges us to recognize and remember the risen Christ in all of the bodies of creation groaning and aching for liberation from the powers of sin and oppression. In an age when human consumption, pollution, and population growth threatens countless numbers of species with extinction and endangers the survival of entire ecosystems, being part of the Body of Christ means learning to hear the cries of the poor that are the bodies and body of nature. It means acknowledging that whenever we failed to honor the goodness and sanctity of the bodies and body of the cosmos, we failed to honor the Body of Christ.

Indeed, because of the interdependence of all the bodies of creation, standing with the wounded bodies and body of nature is one of the most important ways we have of standing with the bodies of the poor, and vice versa. For it is precisely in standing with the poor that we protect the bodies of nature, and in caring for our co-creatures that we create a safe place and viable future for the poor. Poverty, which is both a major cause and consequence of environmental degradation, "is the planet's main 'environmental' problem."[65] When we fail to stand with the poor we force them to overtax and burden the body of creation, and when we fail to tend to the bodies and body of creation it is inevitably the poor that must bear the major burden for our environmental sins. All too often the poor are shoved and squeezed into the most degraded environments, forced to labor under the most environmentally disastrous conditions, and pressured to further deplete and degrade these environments simply to stay alive.

Recognizing our kinship with the bodies and body of creation calls us foremost to live more simply and lightly upon the earth. Just as our solidarity with the wounded Body of Christ, that is the poor, means that we must embrace a spirit of voluntary poverty, so too our fellowship with all the other bodies of creation means that we must live in ways that make room for all of God's creatures and that leave enough space, food, and resources for all the bodies of the planet and cosmos. We need to start living within our environmental means, and to take steps to reduce and eventually eliminate national and global patterns of "deficit spending" of creation's bounty. For those of us in developed nations that means we need to make radical changes in our consumption of energy and other resources, and embrace a simplicity of life that makes room for all the bodies and body of creation.

Conclusion

In the Eucharist we share in and celebrate our identity and vocation as the Body of Christ. The author of Luke reports that the first disciples came to recognize and remember the risen Christ in the breaking of the bread, and in the earliest writings on the Eucharist Paul calls the Christian community in Corinth to recognize the Body of Christ not merely in the bread and wine but also in the community gathered around the table—and particularly in the wounded flesh of the poor. So we read in Acts that the eucharistic community that saw itself formed into a body in the breaking of the bread felt obliged to live as one body, sharing everything in common and tending to the needs and sufferings of their weakest members. Celebrating the Eucharist today, we too are called to "recognize the body" by caring for and standing with all the bodies that make up the wounded Body of Christ and by overcoming all the divisions and injustices that wound that body.

Notes

[1] William Shakespeare, *The Merchant of Venice,* ed. Jay L. Halio, *The Oxford Shakespeare,* ed. Jay L. Halio (Oxford, England: Clarendon Press, 1993) 161–62.

[2] Beverly Wildung Harrison, *Our Right to Choose: Toward a New Ethic of Abortion* (Boston: Beacon, 1983) 106.

[3] Susan A. Ross, "God's Embodiment and Women: Sacraments," in *Freeing Theology: The Essentials of Theology in Feminist Perspective,* ed. Catherine Mowry LaCugna (San Francisco: HarperSanFrancisco: 1993) 186.

[4] Gerard Manley Hopkins, "God's Grandeur," found in *The Norton Anthology of English Literature*, vol. 2, ed. M. H. Abrams et al., rev. ed. (New York: W. W. Norton, 1968) 1433.

[5] Michael J. Himes and Kenneth R. Himes, O.F.M. "The Sacrament of Creation: Toward an Environmental Theology," *Commonweal,* 26 January 1990, 43.

[6] Ross, "God's Embodiment and Women," 186, 198.

[7] Vatican II, "The Pastoral Constitution on the Church in the Modern World," in *Catholic Social Thought: The Documentary Heritage,* ed. David O'Brien and Thomas Shannon (Maryknoll, N.Y.: Orbis, 1997).

[8] Sallie McFague, *The Body of God: An Ecological Theology* (Minneapolis: Fortress, 1993) 164–65.

[9] Ibid., 164.

[10] Susan A. Ross, "'Then Honor God in Your Body' (1 Cor. 6:20): Feminist and Sacramental Theology on the Body," *Horizons* 16 (1989) 7–27; Ross, "Body," in *The New Dictionary of Catholic Spirituality,* ed. Michael Downey (Collegeville: The Liturgical Press, 1993) 93–100; Ross, "God's Embodiment and Women: Sacraments," in *Freeing Theology,* ed. LaCugna, 185–209; Ross, "Body and Gender in Sacramental Theology," in *Extravagant Affections: A Feminist Sacramental Theology,* (New York: Continuum, 2001) 97–136.

[11] Ross, "Body," 94.

[12] Ibid.

[13] Ross, *Extravagant Affections,* 102–3.

[14] Ibid., 108–11.

[15] Peter E. Fink, "Perceiving the Presence of Christ," *Worship* 58 (1984) 17.

[16] Fink, "Perceiving the Presence of Christ," 18.

[17] Eugene LaVerdiere, S.S.S., *Dining in the Kingdom of God* (Chicago, Ill.: Liturgy Training Publications, 1994) 139.

[18] Ibid., 190.

[19] Bernard J. Lee, S.M., "Body of Christ," in *The New Dictionary of Catholic Spirituality,* ed. Michael Downey, 102.

[20] Kenneth R. Himes, "Eucharist and Justice; Assessing the Legacy of Virgil Michel," *Worship* 62 (1988) 203–6.

[21] Paul Hanly Furfey, "Liturgy and the Social Problem," in *National Liturgical Week: Held at the Cathedral of St. Paul and the Catholic Youth Center, St. Paul, Minnesota, October 6–10, 1941* (Newark, N.J.: Benedictine Liturgical Conference, 1942) 185.

[22] R. Kevin Seasoltz, "Justice and the Eucharist," *Worship* 58 (1984) 515.

[23] McFague, *The Body of God,* 164.

[24] Lee, "Body of Christ," 102.

[25] Christine Pohl, *Making Room: Recovering Hospitality as a Christian Tradition* (Grand Rapids, Mich.: Eeerdmans, 1999) 41–48; William R. Crockett, *Eucharist: Symbol of Transformation,* (New York: Pueblo, 1989) 255.

[26] Cited in Crockett, *Symbol of Transformation,* 255.

[27] Robert Ellsberg, ed., *By Little and By Little: The Selected Writings of Dorothy Day* (New York: Knopf, 1983) 330.

[28] For a fuller treatment of the call to simplicity see Duane Elgin, *Voluntary Simplicity,* rev. ed. (New York: Quill, 1993); Latin American Episcopal Council, "The Medellin Document on Poverty of the Church," in *The Gospel of Peace and Justice: Catholic Social Teaching Since Pope,* ed. Joseph Gremillion (Maryknoll, N.Y.: Orbis, 1976) 474–76.

[29] John F. Kavanaugh, *Following Christ in a Consumer Culture: The Spirituality of Cultural Resistance,* rev. ed. (Maryknoll, N.Y.: Orbis, 1991) 3–19.

[30] M. Therese Lysaught, "Eucharist as Basic Training: The Body as Nexus of Liturgy and Ethics," in *Theology and Lived Christianity,* ed. David M. Hammond, ed., (Mystic, Conn.: Twenty-Third Publications, 2000) 266–67.

[31] Christine Gudorf, *Body, Sex and Pleasure: Reconstructing Christian Sexual Ethics* (Cleveland, Ohio: Pilgrim Press, 1994) 11–12.

[32] Ibid., 58; Karen Jo Torjesen, *When Women Were Priests: Women's Leadership in the Early Church & the Scandal of Their Subordination in the Rise of Christianity* (San Francisco: HarperSanFrancisco, 1993) 33.

[33] Raymond F. Collins, *Sexual Ethics and the New Testament: Behavior and Belief* (New York: Herder & Herder, 2000) 186–87; Lisa Sowle Cahill, *Sex, Gender, and Christian Ethics* (New York: Cambridge University Press, 1996) 150–60.

[34] Christine E. Gudorf, "Sexism," in *The New Dictionary of Catholic Social Thought,* ed. Judith A. Dwyer (Collegeville: The Liturgical Press, 1994) 877–81.

[35] Augustine, *De Trinitate,* 12.7.10 from *The Trinity,* trans. Stephen McKenna, C.Ss.R., Fathers of the Church: A New Translation, ed. Roy Joseph Deferrari, vol. 45 (Washington, D.C.: Catholic University of America Press, 1963) 351–53; Aquinas, *Summa Theologiae,* 1.92.1 ad 1 (New York: McGraw Hill, 1964) vol. 13, 35–39; Pius XI, *Casti Connubii,* in *Acta Apostolicae Sedis* 22 (1930) 539–92; Ross, "Then Honor God in Your Body," 10–11.

[36] Christine E. Gudorf, "The Power to Create: Sacraments and Men's Need to Birth," *Horizons* 14 (1987) 296.

[37] Teresa Berger, "Women as Alien Bodies in the Body of Christ? The Place of Women in Worship," in *Liturgy and the Body,* ed. Louis-Marie Chauvet and Francois Kabasele Lumbala, Concilium (London/Philadelphia), 1995/3 (Maryknoll, N.Y.: Orbis, 1995) 114–15.

[38] For two moving accounts of some of the ways women have experienced discrimination and oppression see J. Milburn Thompson, *Justice & Peace: A Christian Primer* (Maryknoll, N.Y.: Orbis, 1997) 98–102; and Lisa Sowle Cahill, *Sex, Gender & Christian Ethics,* 51–55.

[39] Anne Carr, "Women, Justice, and the Church," *Horizons* 17 (1990) 275.

[40] Christine Firer Hinze, "Dirt and Economic Inequality: A Christian-Ethical Peek Under the Rug," *Annual of the Society of Christian Ethics* 21 (2000) 45–62.

[41] United Nations Human Development Programme, *Human Development Report 2001* (New York: Oxford University Press, 2001) 214, 226.

[42] Bishop Jorge Mejia, "The Roots of Violence Against Women," *Origins,* 4 November 1993, 369.

[43] Elizabeth Schüssler Fiorenza and Mary Shawn Copeland, eds., *Violence Against Women,* Concilium (London/Philadelphia), 1994/1 (Maryknoll, N.Y.: Orbis, 1994) x–xvii. See also Catholic Church, Assemblée des évêques du Québec, Comité épiscopal des affaires sociales, *A Heritage of Violence?: A Pastoral Reflection on Conjugal Violence,* trans. Antoinette Kinlough (Montréal: Social Affairs Committee of the Assembly of Quebec Bishops, 1990).

[44] U.S. Catholic Bishops, "Partners in the Mystery of Redemption: A Pastoral Concerns to Women's Concerns for Church and Society," *Origins,* 21 April 1988, 763.

[45] Christine E. Gudorf, "Western Religion and the Patriarchal Family," in *Feminist Ethics and the Catholic Tradition,* ed. Charles E. Curran, Margaret A. Farley, and Richard A. McCormick (New York: Paulist, 1996) 262.

[46] Thompson, *Justice & Peace,* 100.

[47] U.S. Catholic Bishops, "When I Call for Help: Domestic Violence Against Women," *Origins,* 5 November 1992, 355.

[48] Fiorenza and Copeland, *Violence Against Women,* viii.

[49] Thompson, *Justice & Peace,* 100.

[50] Margaret R. Miles, "Religion and Food: The Case of Eating Disorders," *Journal of the American Academy of Religion* 63 (1995) 554.

[51] Ibid., 555.

[52] Abby Ellin, "Dad, Do You Think I Look Too Fat?" *New York Times,* 17 September 2000, 9.

[53] Claudia Kalb, "Our Quest to Be Perfect," *Newsweek,* 16 August 1999, 33.

[54] Mary D. Pellauer, "Pornography: An Agenda for the Churches," in *Sexuality and the Sacred: Sources for Theological Reflection,* ed. James B. Nelson and Sandra P. Longfellow (Louisville, Ky.: Westminster/John Knox Press, 1994) 345–53.

[55] Carol Smolenski, "Sex Tourism and the Sexual Exploitation of Children," *Christian Century,* 15 November 1995, 1079–81; Martha Neff-Smith, Gale Spencer, and Valerie R. Tavai, "AIDS in Asia: Linking Tragedy in Thailand and Myanmar," *Journal of Multicultural Nursing and Health* 7 (2000) 17–20.

[56] James Nash, *Loving Nature: Ecological Integrity and Christian Responsibility* (Nashville, Tenn.: Abingdon, 1991) 72.

[57] Lynn White, "The Historical Roots of Our Ecological Crisis," *Science* 10 (March 1967) 1203–7. For a Christian response to this challenge see Nash, *Loving Nature,* 68–92.

[58] Elizabeth A. Johnson, *Women, Earth, and Creator Spirit* (Mahwah, N.J.: Paulist, 1993) 29.

[59] Carolyn Merchant, *Radical Ecology: The Search for a Livable World* (New York: Routledge, 1992) 42–44, 46; Larry Rasmussen, *Earth Community, Earth Ethics* (Maryknoll, N.Y.: Orbis, 1996) 58.

[60] U.S. Catholic Bishops, "Renewing the Earth: An Invitation to Reflection and Action on the Environment in Light of Catholic Social Teaching," *Origins,* 12 December 1991, 429. See also, Pope John Paul II, "Peace with All Creation,"

Origins, 14 December 1989, 465–68; The Evangelical Lutheran Church in America, "Caring for Creation: Vision, Hope and Justice," September 1993, http://www.elca.org/dcs/environment.html, 2.

[61] McFague, *The Body of God,* 164.

[62] Johnson, *Women, Earth, and Creator Spirit,* 30.

[63] Lee, "Body of Christ," 104.

[64] Himes and Himes, "The Sacrament of Creation," 43–44.

[65] Nash, *Loving Nature,* 50.

Chapter Four

An Unbloody Sacrifice

The Sacrifice of the Mass

For most of us growing up in the Catholic Church before Vatican II, the Eucharist was the Mass and the Mass was "the unbloody sacrifice of the body and blood of Christ."[1] Back then we may not have thought of the Eucharist as a sacrament of eating and drinking, nor paid much attention to the radical table fellowship to which Jesus was calling us to in the breaking of the bread. And we may not have always remembered that the congregation gathered around this table was as much the Body of Christ as the bread and wine being blessed and broken. But every Catholic girl and boy knew that the Mass was a sacrifice.

Like any sacrifice, the Mass was offered (not celebrated) by a priest at an altar. The priest who offered the holy and unbloody sacrifice of the Mass on our behalf was our mediator, a bridge between those of us kneeling in the pews and God up in Heaven. So both the priest and the altar on which this sacrifice was offered were set apart from the rest of us. Only the priest (accompanied by some altar boys) went into the sacred space of the sanctuary on the other side of the Communion rail and ascended the steps to the altar pressed against the back wall of the church. Only the priest wore special vestments reminding us that he was acting *in persona Christi* or spoke in a foreign tongue that only God and other priests seemed to understand. And, with his back to the congregation and his eyes lifted to heaven, only the priest could say the Mass and hold the consecrated offerings in his sacred hands. There may have been bread and wine consumed at Mass, but few of us thought we were in church for a meal or fellowship. Reading along in our missals, we knew we were there to assist in the Mass by attentively watching and hearing the sacrifice being offered in our name.

As we learned in our catechisms and read in our missals, in every Mass the perfect and bloody sacrifice of Christ on the cross was made present to us in an unbloody fashion, and through the priest at the altar we somehow shared in this original and unique sacrifice and benefited from its redemptive graces. On the cross Christ had died once and for all for our sins, and Christ offered the perfect and unrepeatable sacrifice to God in heaven. Still, in some mysterious but real way the sacrifice of the cross was re-presented to us in the sacrifice of the Mass. Indeed, though their manner was different (the cross was a bloody sacrifice in which Christ was slain, while the Mass was an unbloody sacrifice in which Christ did not die again), they were one sacrifice. "For the victim [Christ] is one and the same: the same [Christ] now offers through the ministry of priests, who then offered himself on the cross."[2]

For centuries the language of sacrifice dominated our understanding of the Mass and of the mystery of Christ's death and resurrection which it re-presented to us. In spite of the fact that we understood the Mass or Eucharist as a memorial of the Last Supper and spoke of the Eucharist as Holy Communion, when we thought of the Mass it was not primarily as food or meal or Body of Christ, but as sacrifice. We understood Christ's death and resurrection first and foremost as a sacrificial offering that transcended every other sacrifice offered down through the ages and won our redemption and salvation by making peace with the God we had offended thorough our sinfulness. At the Last Supper and on the cross Christ was both our high priest and our sacrificial offering, the one true priest who interceded for us by offering the perfect and unblemished sacrifice to God, and the Lamb of God who was the willing and spotless victim of this sacrifice and whose innocent death washed away our sins. And so we saw the Mass, which was the memorial of this sacrifice, as a sacrifice as well, a real sacrifice in which Christ (through the action of the priest) transformed our meager gifts of bread and wine into an offering of his body and blood, and in so doing joined us to that sublime sacrifice that had won our salvation and atoned for our sins.

This notion of atonement or satisfaction (traditional theology used words like "expiation" and "propitiation") was at the center of

our understanding of the cross and the Mass as sacrifice. For we saw
Christ's death on the cross not so much as liberation or deliverance
from the power of sin, but as a sacrifice satisfying or canceling the
debt we owed God because of our sins.[3] As generations of Catholics
learned from their *Baltimore Catechism*, a central purpose of Christ's
sacrifice was to "satisfy God's justice" for our sins, to placate God's
righteous wrath and make amends for the offense of our sins. Through
our sinful disobedience we had wronged God and humanity stood
guilty before the almighty judge and lawgiver. God, who was com-
passionate, was prepared to forgive us, but first it was necessary that
our sins be atoned for. And because the one we offended was perfect,
we required a perfect sacrifice to cancel the debt incurred. We needed
a holy and unblemished lamb. Indeed, our offense could only be forgiven if the sacrifice offered in our name was divine. And so only the
death of Christ would do.

Christ's sacrifice on the cross and in the Mass washed away the
stain of our sin and made amends for the offense we had given God.
In this way our guilt as sinners was removed and God's justice satisfied. The death of Christ on the cross (and re-presented in the Mass)
had paid our debt. As we pray to God in Eucharistic Prayer II, "We
offer you in thanksgiving this holy and living *sacrifice* (emphasis
added). . . . See the Victim who has reconciled us to yourself."
Christ's sacrifice secured God's forgiveness and canceled our debt as
sinners. And the Mass or Eucharist memorialized and re-presented
that sacrifice to us and allowed us to present this perfect offering to
God's altar in heaven.

The one sacrifice of the cross and the Mass, then, had made our
peace with God. The violent death of Christ on the cross had satisfied
the debt owed to God, washed away the guilt of our sins, and reconciled us to the one we had wronged. The bloody sacrifice of an innocent victim had secured God's forgiveness and bought our peace.
Again, as we pray in Eucharistic Prayer II, "Lord, may this sacrifice,
which has made our peace with you, advance the peace and salvation
of the whole world."

Today we continue to describe the Eucharist as a sacrifice and to
affirm that in this memorial meal the sacrifice of Christ on the cross
is somehow made present, and that "the sacrifice of Christ and the
sacrifice of the Eucharist are *one single sacrifice* (emphasis original)."[4]
Still, sacrifice is no longer the central or guiding metaphor we use to

describe the Eucharist or the primary paradigm for speaking about Christ's death and resurrection. We hardly ever hear about the "unbloody sacrifice of the Mass" any more, and there has been a recovery of a number of other metaphors and images to speak about the Eucharist.

We talk about the Eucharist as "the breaking of the bread," "the Lord's Table" or "the Lord's Supper," describe it as a banquet or a feast celebrated in remembrance of all Christ's meals and in anticipation of the heavenly banquet, and we generally focus on the nature of the Eucharist as a meal.[5] And with these changes in language have come changes in our experience and understanding of the Eucharist. Latin and the Communion rail are gone. There are more of us in the sanctuary, and the altar (now often called a table) has been moved away from the wall so the priest celebrant can face us as we celebrate the Eucharist together. Church architecture and liturgical reforms have made more room for the congregation and reinforced the notion of the Eucharist as a meal, and we have a stronger sense of being a community gathered to celebrate our identity and vocation as Christ's body and less of a sense of being silent observers of a sacrificial rite.

Still, even in its diminished capacity the notion of the Eucharist and Christ's death and resurrection as sacrifice seems troubling to a number of Christian thinkers. What does it mean to say, many wonder, that sinful humanity could only be reconciled to God through the violent death of an innocent person? What are we saying about God when we affirm that the Almighty's sense of justice demanded that such a violent sacrifice be offered in order to satisfy our outstanding debt? What sort of God are we imaging here? A God who can or must be placated by violence? Is this vision of a God who demands (or even accepts) human sacrifice consistent with the God we find in Scripture or Christian theology? And what are we saying to all the victims of violence and injustice when we teach that God required or accepted the death of an innocent victim as payment for our sins? Are we encouraging passivity in the face of institutional violence and all forms of victimization? Are we teaching the poor and oppressed and marginalized and tortured to embrace their role as victims?

If the language of sacrifice is to be helpful in describing the mystery of Christ's death and resurrection or the sacrament of the Eucharist, we will need to reexamine just what we mean by this metaphor. We will need to ask what it means to say that this violent sacrifice was the instrument of peace reconciling God and humanity, and we will need to ask what the sacrifice of Christ calls us to do and be as disciples who celebrate the Eucharist in remembrance of him. And so in this chapter we will ask just what it means to speak about the Eucharist as a sacrifice, and in what way the sacrifice of the cross can be described as a sign of peace between God and humanity—and a summons to peace among all peoples. We live in a world immersed in violence and often dangerously close to being overwhelmed by that violence. If the memorial of the execution of an innocent person is to be seen as the path to peace and reconciliation in such a world and not the baptism of such violence we must ask just what Christians mean when we describe our central sacrament as a sacrifice.

The Problem of Sacrifice

People in nearly every culture and religion have made sacrifices to their gods. Sometimes the gifts have been a portion of the harvest or an animal culled from the herd. Not infrequently human beings have been sacrificed. In either case, the sacrificial offering was to be a gift to the god or gods, expressing thanks or praise, or seeking some manner of favor or forgiveness. On some level sacrifices have been an attempt to secure or restore a good relationship with the realm of the divine.[6] For both ancient and modern peoples the world is often experienced as an uncertain and dangerous place, filled with powers and forces beyond our understanding and control, and sacrifice has been seen as one way to befriend or appease the mysteries we cannot control.[7]

In *Violence and the Sacred,* however, anthropologist René Girard has argued that humans have not offered sacrifices (especially human sacrifices) to please the gods, but to stem a plague of human violence that is always on the brink of annihilating civilization.[8] Indeed, Girard argues that ancient religions used the sacred violence of sacrifice to keep human communities from being torn apart by the myriad of hostilities and rivalries bubbling beneath the surface of every society, or from being swamped by the escalating cycle of vengeance set off by any act of violence.[9]

According to Girard, human communities are constantly threatened with two forms of violence, and ancient religions used the sacred violence of human (and then animal) sacrifice to prevent these dual

types of violence from overwhelming and disintegrating their societies. First, every society needed to defend its union against the slings
and arrows of all the hostilities and rivalries that fester in any human
community. Our desire to possess our neighbor's goods, fortune, or
spouse; our greed, envy, selfishness, and lust; our love of power and
wish to dominate others—all of these set us on a collision course with
those around us and generate countless resentments and divisions
tearing at the fabric of society. And second, when these hostilities boil
over into an act of violence, we find ourselves sucked into an escalating cycle of vengeance. An eye must be had for an eye, a limb for a
limb, until, as Gandhi noted, we are all blind and lame. With a logic
both relentless and insane, strike leads to counterstrike, and one
avenged slaying is matched and then exceeded by the killing of others
until the whole community is destroyed.

Human sacrifices, Girard argued, solved the problem of a community being torn apart by a plague of hostilities and rivalries by fo-
cusing all this divisive violence on a single sacrificial victim. When
members of a community found one common victim to take on all
the accumulated annoyances and animosities they felt towards one
another, there was suddenly a new sense of solidarity and communion.
In their shared violence towards this victim, people were distracted
from all the tensions and trials of their life together and felt at least
temporarily purged of the grievances and grudges tearing at their
community. In the sacred violence of human sacrifice the society that
had been teetering on the brink of dissolution was suddenly renewed
by its shared hostility to the sacrificial victim. He or she had become
their scapegoat, and had carried away the sins alienating them from
one another. The sacrificial victim's death had purchased a sort of
peace for the community, but a peace built on violence.

The sacrificial victim was also the solution to the problem of
vengeance, which was forever threatening to swamp human communities in a rising tide of blood. The trouble with vengeance was that
violence always invited a reactive violence from the victim's family or
tribe, and this tit-for-tat approach had no way of short-circuiting itself,
particularly in primitive societies without a recognized judicial system.
So, one act of violence led to an endless chain of vengeance. Murder
begat murder, which, in turn, begat more murder.

But, Girard argued, if a victim could be found whose death would
satisfy the bloodlust let loose by violence, but not trigger more re-

active violence, this killing might break the cycle of vengeance. For if the mounting rage of the blood feud tearing the community apart could be expressed through the death of an innocent party, who was not a member of either group, this sacrifice would satisfy the need for revenge while short-circuiting the cycle of vengeance. Once again the sacrificial victim would purchase peace for the community by being killed.

Still, the sacred violence of sacrifice would only work as a tonic to the human violence threatening to tear communities apart as long as its practitioners were not aware of what they were doing. Girard argued that sacrifice succeeded because communities could hide from the violence they were perpetrating against innocent persons by claiming that this violence was required by the gods.[10] Humans were not killing innocent persons in order to distract themselves from the hostilities and rivalries in their own hearts or to satisfy and short-circuit some murderous lust for vengeance. Societies were not putting these victims to death to purchase peace among their members. Rather, sacrifices had been commanded by the gods, and these victims were being slain to satisfy the violence and appease the wrath of deities, not humans.

The sacrificial process described by Girard only worked if communities kept two secrets from themselves: that everyone was responsible for the hostilities and rivalries tearing at the fabric of their society, and that they were purchasing a peace of sorts by the violent death of innocent persons. Scapegoating only worked if communities could maintain the myth of their collective innocence and righteousness, and this was only possible if they could blame the sacrificial victim for their hostilities and rivalries and the gods for their sacrificial violence. Otherwise, they would have to acknowledge that their scapegoating did not address the underlying causes of violence in their hearts or community, and that their sacrifice was a cruel and unjust act of violence—meant not to appease the wrath of gods but of humans.

Modern society, Girard notes, has eliminated the religious practice of human sacrifice and found other ways to address human violence and the threat of vengeance. Instead of relying on religious cults or victims' families to stem the tide of revenge, we have judicial systems that punish offenders on behalf of the state. Only the government may inflict penalties or take lives, and its use of force is intended to satisfy the need for justice without triggering further violence.

Still, the sacrificial victim has not completely lost its appeal. We continue to be attracted to the idea that someone else can be blamed for life's woes—especially for our part in these troubles—and human communities everywhere are still mesmerized by the intoxicating sense of unity and solidarity that comes with finding a common foe or victim on whom to unleash all our complaints and grievances. Without offering human sacrifices on our religious altars, we still make scapegoats of others, hoping to escape the burdens of living in community with lots of equally frail human beings by finding one or two victims to carry the guilt.

Since it does little good to look at the scapegoats of others (as this only makes us feel innocent and righteous, allowing us to scapegoat these other communities), we will look at some of the ways in which our own Christian community and contemporary society have scapegoated and sacrificed victims.

Our Scapegoats

Though there are other examples of Christian scapegoating, the story of Christianity has been marred in a particular way by our scapegoating of Jews and women. For two millennia Christians have unfairly blamed and punished the Jewish faith and people for the death of Christ, scapegoating Jews for the universal sinfulness and violence of the human community.[11] Since the time of Constantine, Christian Europe has discriminated against, harassed, and oppressed Jews, treating them with suspicion, hostility, and often violent injustice. And during most of that time, the Christian Church has propagated anti-Semitic distortions and propaganda that ignored Jesus' identity as a faithful Jew. The Christian Church justified and encouraged prejudice, persecutions, and pogroms of every sort, leading finally to the ultimate horror of the Holocaust. Only in the twentieth century has there been any acknowledgment of the injustice and sinfulness of this scapegoating.[12]

Women too have been a favorite scapegoat of Christianity. As we have seen elsewhere, Christian theology long described women as morally, intellectually, physically, and spiritually inferior to men. Because a patriarchal and sexist Church and society identified women more closely with their bodies and sexuality than men, they were judged to be more carnal and sinful creatures. Like Eve, burdened with an unfair and disproportionate share of the blame for humanity's fall from grace, women have been portrayed as sensual, seductive, and morally dangerous temptresses, needing to be controlled and dominated by a man.

This scapegoating of women helped to justify the marginalization and oppression of women in and out of the Church, denying women equality as co-disciples, excluding them from leadership roles, and marginalizing them in Christian worship. Women were not Christlike enough to preside at the Eucharist, and so they were excluded from the sanctuary. Even worse, this scapegoating has encouraged and justified to a murderous plague of domestic violence that has been the scourge of women and girls in every society and age. Even the Vatican acknowledges that "violence against women has as its root cause a . . . conviction that women are not equal to men,"[13] and far too many males learned this conviction from their church.[14]

An essential part of the scapegoating of women has been to hold them responsible for the consequences of our shared sexual sins and failings, and to blame them for sexual crimes committed against them. Whether we are talking about premarital sex, adultery, sexual harassment, or rape, the tendency has all too often been to place the blame on the woman.

In John 7:53–8:11 a woman who has been "caught in the very act of committing adultery" (8:4) is brought before Jesus to be condemned, but her partner (who must have been present when she was apprehended) is absent, unknown, and unaccused. In the eyes of her accusers it would seem that she alone has committed this sin, and that only she needs to be punished. And in John 4:5-42 Jesus encounters a Samaritan woman who has been ostracized for her sexual sins, but there is no evidence that any of her male partners suffered any stigma or punishment for their indiscretions.

From these unnamed women to Hester Prynne of *The Scarlet Letter* and today's unwed mothers, women continue to be scapegoated for extramarital sexuality. Indeed, in our contemporary society the scapegoating of women includes blaming single mothers for an economy that has trapped one-fifth of our children in poverty. For more than three decades the real wages of blue-collar workers in this country have stagnated or declined, forcing most families to send both parents into the labor force and cut savings to the bone. But when politicians and pundits identify a culprit behind this long-term financial malaise, they invariably turn to all those single mothers "on the dole." Poverty, we are told, will be eliminated by getting single mothers to work at menial jobs.[15]

For far too long women have also been scapegoated for the sexual sins committed against them, including sexual harassment, incest, rape, and domestic violence. The victims of these crimes have been asked what they did to provoke the harassment or violence directed against them. They have been told that they dressed or behaved too provocatively, that they invited the unwanted attention or attack of their abuser or assailant. They had been too friendly—or not friendly and obedient enough. And they have been encouraged to forgive and forget, not to press charges or ruin someone's promising career or good name.

Still, women have not been the only sexual scapegoats. Homosexuals too have been scapegoated by the larger society. Until very recently homosexual persons have made up an invisible or "closeted" community in our society, with most living anonymously among their heterosexual siblings and neighbors. In *The Nature of Prejudice,* psychologist Gordon Allport explains this self-imposed invisibility by noting that homosexual persons are the objects of some of our culture's most virulent prejudice, and that they would suffer even graver violence if they could be identified and targeted by the larger community.[16] This argument is borne out by the increased reports of "gay bashing," sexual harassment, and hate crimes committed against homosexual persons since many began to come out of the closet over the last two decades.

In spite of the fact the psychiatry no longer describes homosexuality as an impairment or disease, homosexuals continue to be stereotyped as promiscuous, unbalanced, immature, or even dangerous sexual predators. Throughout the 1980s homosexuals were blamed for the AIDS epidemic, which a number of Church leaders saw as an expression of God's wrath against gays and drug addicts. More recently, homosexuals have been made the scapegoats for nearly everything that is wrong with contemporary society. In *Heterosexism,* Patricia Beattie Jung and Ralph Smith note that homosexuals have been blamed for undermining family values, weakening the fabric of society, discouraging procreation, confusing adolescents, and preying on the vulnerable. Beattie and Smith establish the error of all these accusations, noting in particular that "all of the evidence points to the fact that most sexual abuse of children is perpetrated by heterosexual males."[17] Still, the scapegoating continues. In the recent priest pedophilia scandal, not a few Church leaders suggested that the problem was a high percentage of homosexuals in the clergy.

There has also been a significant amount of scapegoating in America's ongoing wars on crime and drugs, repeatedly targeting our nation's poor and minorities and requiring them to bear the brunt of the blame for the crime and violence in our society, as well as the underlying social ills that create these problems. Since 1972 America's most recent war on crime has resulted in the sextupling of our prison population. With more than 2 million people behind bars and nearly 4 million on parole or probation, America is the now world's leading jailer, imprisoning about one-half million more people than China and holding one-quarter of all the world's prisoners in its cells. And the vast majority of these prisoners are poor and minorities.

As criminologist Elliott Currie has argued in *Crime and Punishment in America,* for the past few decades our society has abandoned its war on poverty in favor of a war on crime, which has mainly been a war against the poor. "While we were busily jamming our prisons to the rafters with young, poor men, we were simultaneously . . . tolerating the descent of several millions of Americans, most of them children, into poverty."[18] A 1996 report of the National Criminal Justice Commission noted that our nation "was spending billions of dollars to lock up hundreds of thousands of people while at the same time cutting billions of dollars for programs that would provide opportunity for young Americans." As a result, America now has the industrialized world's highest rates of incarceration and poverty, and the greatest gap between its rich and poor.[19] Instead of addressing the underlying causes of crime and violence in our society, we have sacrificed millions of our poor to a prison-industrial complex that has not made our neighborhoods safer or our society more peaceful.[20]

Our drug wars too have scapegoated the poor and minorities. Drug historian David Musto's *The American Disease: Origins of Narcotic Control* points out that in the nineteenth and twentieth centuries America's drug wars regularly scapegoated minorities like the Chinese (opium), Mexicans (marijuana), and blacks (cocaine), prosecuting and imprisoning these groups because they had become an economic or political threat.[21] Other critics add that America's current war on drugs and crime has primarily been a war against the poor and minorities, targeting inner-city neighborhoods where they live. Michel Tonry notes that "the lives of black and Hispanic ghetto kids have been sacrificed in order to reinforce white kids' norms against drugs."[22] Indeed, "although the prevalence of drug use among white men is approximately the same as that among black men, black men are five times as likely to be arrested for a drug offense," and seven times as likely to be imprisoned.[23] As a result, African Americans now make up more than one-half of America's convict population.

Clearly, then, the use of sacrificial victims and scapegoats is not dead in modern society. But how does this practice of sacrifice fit with what Christ did—and with what we do with Christ—in the Eucharist?

"Mercy, Not Sacrifice"

According to Girard, primitive religion used sacrifice to stem the tide of human violence forever threatening to swamp and overwhelm their societies, while maintaining the myth that these sacrificial victims were being offered to placate the wrath of the gods. Thus, ancient religion and its sacrificial rituals were used to keep communities unaware of the violence lurking within them and threatening to tear them apart. In the sacrificial system this very human violence was projected onto the victim (who deserved to die) and the gods (who demanded this sacred violence).

Sacrifice, then, presumes a deity who demands or accepts scapegoats, a god whose wrath or sense of justice needs to be placated or appeased by the death of innocent victims. But is this the God we find in the Bible? Is the God who is revealed to us in the Scriptures: a being who grants peace to those who offer up scapegoats? Girard and a growing number of Christian theologians think not.[24] Indeed, Girard argues that the Bible unmasks the myth of sacred violence underlying the practices of sacrifice and scapegoating, and it reveals a God who opposes scapegoating and stands with the world's sacrificial victims scapegoats. Here is a God, who, as Jesus reminds us in Matthew 9:13, desires "mercy, not sacrifice" (see Hosea 6:6).

There clearly are sacrifices offered to and accepted by God in the Scriptures, and a number of biblical characters see their scapegoating of others as mandated by God. But for Girard the uniqueness of the Bible is that there are so many stories within it that resist and expose the myth of sanctioned violence. For him the Bible's revelatory character is to be found in its increasing aversion to the sacred violence of sacrifice and its deepening commitment to remember human history from the perspective of its scapegoats and victims.[25] As Louis-Marie Chauvet notes:

> the Bible is unique in this, God takes the part of sacrificed victims (and from the very beginning as the story of Abel testifies) and as a consequence, instead of 'blessing' a group that is cheaply reconciled by the use of a sacralized victim, God charges the group to take in hand its ethical responsibility toward such victims: the immigrant, the slave, the orphan, and so on.[26]

As we will see below, far from sanctioning the sacred violence of sacrifice, Scripture reveals a God who opposes scapegoating and stands with the sacrificial victims—indeed, a God who identifies with all of history's scapegoats and becomes the ultimate victim, thus unmasking the diabolical violence that would pass itself off as divine.

The God of the Scapegoats

Scripture's revelation of a God who is opposed to scapegoating begins in Genesis. In the garden the first couple is given permission to eat of every tree, "but of the tree of the knowledge of good and evil you shall not eat" (2:17). But the man and woman are not satisfied being mere mortals and covet what they see as the divine power to draw a line between good and evil. So they take of the forbidden fruit, and when confronted by God they begin immediately to cast blame, each hoping to maintain their own innocence by accusing the other. The man, who had only verses before (2:23) proclaimed that "This at last is bone of my bones and flesh of my flesh" now complains to God that "The woman whom you gave to be with me, she gave me fruit from the tree, and I ate" (3:12). And the woman retorts that "The serpent tricked me, and I ate" (3:13). Suddenly, our ancestors possess the coveted knowledge of good and evil—but it proves to be a diabolical and not a divine understanding.

The biblical narrative exposes the cowardice, cruelty, and dishonesty of scapegoating, and it acknowledges that the human community has been sundered by this attempt to sacrifice another on the altar of our innocence. God does not accept such deceitful sin offerings or excuses, and humans lose the peace they had enjoyed with God, with each other, and with the rest of creation.

Genesis again underscores the folly of scapegoating in the tale of Cain and Abel. Cain is jealous of his brother's success and becomes convinced that he will only have peace if this sibling is destroyed. But God will have none of this scapegoating and warns Cain that this desire to blame and kill his brother is related to his own not doing well and to sin "lurking at the door" desiring him (4:7). And when Cain does slay Abel, God does not see it as a blood offering but as murder —and it buys Cain no peace, only anguish.

Nor will God allow Cain to become a scapegoat for others, even though he has murdered his own brother and is hardly an innocent party. Lest anyone think that they can please or placate God by offering up this murderer on an altar of sacrifice, Cain receives a mark or protection "so that no one who came upon him would kill him" (4:15). The violence in the human community will not be excised by killing a killer.

In Genesis 22:1-18 we have the story of Abraham preparing to sacrifice his own son as a sign of his unquestioning obedience and love of God. But it is also a story of God accepting this love while refusing the sacrifice of Abraham's son. In *Violence Unveiled,* Gil Bailie notes that human sacrifice was not unknown in the region where Israel came to flourish, and this story may reflect Israel's own growing renunciation of this practice. According to Bailie, "What we must try to see in the story of Abraham's nonsacrifice of Isaac is that Abraham's faith consisted, not of almost doing what he didn't do, but of *not* doing what he almost did—and not doing it in fidelity to the God in whose name his contemporaries thought it should be done."[27]

The biblical narrative also exposes and rejects the logic of scapegoating in the story of Joseph and his brothers in Genesis 37–48. As with Cain and Abel, sibling rivalry and discontent over the favor shown by their father to this one brother leads the sons of Jacob to plot against Joseph, hoping to find contentment once he has been removed from their midst. But the biblical author is decidedly unsympathetic to their plight and tells the narrative from the perspective of their unjustly scapegoated victim. Later, when the enslaved Joseph has been again scapegoated (this time by his master's wife) God intervenes to rescue him and brings him eventually into the court of the Pharaoh, where he serves as second in command of all Egypt.

Ultimately Joseph proves to be his father and brother's savior, delivering them from starvation and welcoming them into Egypt, and Joseph tells his brothers they should not feel guilty about their behavior towards him (45:5). Still, it is clear from the narrative that the scapegoating of this brother was indeed cruel and unjust, and that the deliverance of Jacob and his children did not result from the sacrifice of an innocent victim but from God's standing with and rescuing this victim from the violence done to him.

In Exodus we encounter a God who sides with the Pharaoh's scapegoats and who delivers them from the sacrificial violence that is enslaving them and slaughtering their children. When a new king ascends to the throne of Egypt, this Pharaoh incites the Egyptians against the Israelites by claiming that the children of Jacob have grown too numerous, prosperous, and powerful, making them a threat to their adopted land. This bit of demagoguery allows the Pharaoh to unite his people in a common cause ("Egypt for the Egyptians"), while feeding his coffers from the robbery and enslavement of his scapegoats. So these immigrants are pressed into forced labor, and when their numbers continue to increase in spite of this oppression, the Pharaoh orders that the Israelites' infant sons should be murdered.

The God of the Bible, however, will not tolerate this scapegoating and does not receive the sacrifice of the Pharaoh as an acceptable offering. Instead, this God is disturbed and haunted by the mournful lament of these Hebrew slaves and announces to Moses that

> I have observed the misery of my people who are in Egypt; I have heard their cry on account of their taskmasters. Indeed, I know their sufferings, and I have come down to deliver them from the Egyptians, and to bring them up out of that land to a good and broad land, a land flowing with milk and honey (Exod 3:7-8).

And so the foundational story of the people of Israel is a tale of God standing with and rescuing a community of scapegoats, of God rejecting the sanctioned violence of sacrifice, exposing it as cruelty and injustice, and coming to the aid of its victims.

Even more amazing, the Bible also reveals this God as one who then stands with the scapegoats of scapegoats. For after the Israelites are rescued from the pharaoh's altar of sacrifice and delivered to a land of their own, they are tempted to forget God's opposition to scapegoating, and they need to be reminded that their God sides with victims and expects them to do the same. Deuteronomy 10:18 reminds the Hebrews that the Lord God "executes justice for the orphan and the widow and who loves the strangers providing them food and clothing," and Jeremiah 22:3-4 relays God's command to "Act with justice and righteousness, and deliver from the hand of the oppressor anyone who has been robbed. And do no wrong or violence to the alien, the orphan, and the widow, or shed innocent blood in this place."

Still, Exodus 22:21-24 may offer the starkest evidence that the God of the Hebrews is a God who stands with and defends scapegoats: "You shall not wrong or oppress a resident alien, for you were aliens in the land of Egypt. You shall not abuse any widow or orphan. If you do abuse them, when they cry out to me, I will surely heed their cry; my wrath will burn, and I will kill you with the sword, and your wives shall become widows and your children orphans."

Scapegoating depends on a kind of amnesia, on forgetting that our victims are people like ourselves, that they are, as Shylock says, "fed with the same food, hurt with the same weapons, subject to the same diseases, [and] healed by the same means."[28] And so God repeatedly reminds the Israelites what they have in common with the potential scapegoats in their midst and commands them to refrain from any injustice against these little ones. "You shall not oppress a resident alien" we read in Exodus 23:9, "you know the heart of an alien, for you were aliens in the land of Egypt." And in Deuteronomy 10:19 the Hebrews are told that "You shall also love the stranger, for you were strangers in the land of Egypt."

Indeed, it is not enough that the Hebrews refrain from abusing or scapegoating the stranger and poor person in their midst. They must, like their God, stand in solidarity with all potential scapegoats and with all of society's victims. As we have seen elsewhere, they are to set aside a portion of their crops for the poor and to offer the poor loans without interest. They are to love the alien as they love themselves, and to come to the aid of widows, orphans, and the poor. And every fifty years they are to cancel all the debts of the poor, let all their indentured servants go free, and give back the poor person's land.

And when they offer sacrifices to their God, they must be offerings acceptable to the God of scapegoats and victims. In Isaiah 1:10-20, God rejects the sacrifices being offered by the Hebrews and commands instead that they show justice to victims and scapegoats. "Bringing offerings is futile; incense is an abomination to me. New moon and sabbath and calling of convocation—I cannot endure solemn assemblies with iniquity. . . . [For] your hands are full of blood" (1:13, 15). In place of such offerings the Israelites are to "learn to do good; seek justice, rescue the oppressed, defend the orphan, plead for the widow" (v. 17). Amos 5:21-24 and Micah 6:1-8 also condemn any sacrifices offered by those who fail to practice justice on behalf of victims.[29] And in Isaiah 58, God promises to bless the Hebrews' offerings only "If you remove the yoke from among you, the pointing of the finger, the speaking of evil, if you offer your food to the hungry and satisfy the needs of the afflicted" (vv. 9-10). The one sacrifice this God desires is an end to scapegoating and justice for all victims.

The God Who Becomes the Scapegoat

If the God revealed to us in the Old Testament sides with scapegoats and increasingly shuns sacrificial offerings, in the New Testament this God takes on the identity of a scapegoat and disarms the violence of scapegoating and vengeance through nonviolence, enemy-love, and forgiveness. The God of the scapegoats becomes a scapegoat, not to satisfy a wrathful and righteous deity, but to liberate us from our own violence. The God to whom sacrifices and scapegoats are supposedly being offered becomes one with all scapegoats and in so doing unmasks the folly of sacrifice and testifies to the immeasurable love of God who will not be turned away by human violence. In Christ, God has taken on our humanity and walked into the heart of human violence, refusing either to flee before the hostile forces being marshaled against him or to respond to this violence with scapegoating or vengeance. The God who has become scapegoat to free us of our own violence will have nothing to do with making new victims.

Christ's whole life is an identification with the world's scapegoats and victims, an act of divine solidarity with the poor, oppressed, and outcast. In Luke's infancy narrative, Jesus, sharing the plight of the poor and the homeless, is born in a stable, "because there was no place for them in the inn" (2:7). And in Matthew's account the Christ child is both a target of the king's murderous violence and a refugee driven into exile, both of these episodes echoing the Pharaoh's scapegoating of the children of Jacob. At the start of his public life in Nazareth, Jesus announces that "The Spirit of the Lord is upon me, because he has anointed me to bring good news to the poor. He has sent me to proclaim release to the captives and recovery of sight to the blind, to let the oppressed go free" (Luke 4:18). And, as we have seen elsewhere, throughout his ministry Jesus repeatedly sides and identifies with those scapegoated and victimized by his own society. In his table fellowship Jesus scandalizes and provokes the righteous by befriending and breaking bread with women, foreigners, tax collectors, and all manner of sinners and in his healing miracles he reaches out to touch the sick, possessed, and unclean of every sort.[30] What's more, he urges his audiences and disciples to show a similar solidarity with society's scapegoats and victims.

We also see this identification with victims and scapegoats in Christ's parables of the heavenly banquet and the kingdom of God. As we noted earlier, in the topsy-turvy world of God's coming reign it is the outcasts and unclean, the beggars and sinners who will be seated first at the heavenly feast. Prostitutes and tax collectors are being given the best seats and the Prodigal Son is being feted with a fatted calf. This is a beggars' banquet, and Christ the physician has come for the sick and the sinners, not for those who only see the splinter in others' eyes. And in the last judgment parable in Matthew 25:31-46, Jesus identifies himself so closely with the poor, hungry, homeless, sick, and imprisoned that anything we do or don't do for one of these little ones is being done or not done for Christ.

Not only does Christ identify with scapegoats and victims, he also exposes and rejects the violence that creates and multiplies them. His solidarity with sinners and outcasts scandalizes those who see themselves as righteous and innocent because he is exposing the hypocrisy and violence of their scapegoating. When the angry mob in John's Gospel is ready to stone the woman caught (alone) in the act of adultery, he suggests that the one among them who is without sin should throw the first stone. When the Pharisee in the Temple (Luke 18:10-14) thanks God that he is not like the sinful tax collector (and when we thank God that we are not like the self-righteous Pharisee), Jesus reminds us that only the repentant tax collector is reconciled with God. When a lawyer wants to know if he has to love Samaritans as neighbors, Jesus tells a parable (Luke 10:25-37) in which the Samaritan proves to be a better neighbor than any Jew (or Christian). And when the offended brother in Luke's parable of the Prodigal Son (15:11-32) complains that his father has been profligate in loving this worthless sinner, the older son is reminded that this sinner is also his brother. As we noted earlier, scapegoating depends on us forgetting that our scapegoats are like us, and Jesus constantly reminds us of that similarity.

And he refuses to be drawn into the spiral of vengeance that is forever making and slaughtering new scapegoats. Instead of offering up more and more sacrifices on the altar of violence and revenge, Christ teaches and practices a nonviolent love of enemies. In the fifth chapter of Matthew we are told that it is not enough to refrain from murder. We must not harbor grudges or call each other names. It is not sufficient that we limit our violence or vengeance to an eye for an eye. We must turn our cheek when struck, give our cloak to the one who demands our shirt, and go two miles with the person who presses us into service for one. Loving our neighbor is not enough. We have to love our enemies and pray for our persecutors. We have to repent of the violence that always seems justified and practice a love that exposes—and short circuits—violence, a love that refuses to make new victims or scapegoats. In the midst of all the violence tearing at the fabric of our hearts and communities, we must remember the humanity of our enemies and love them as ourselves.

Christ's identification with scapegoats and resistance to scapegoating takes on its most complete form in the mystery of his passion and death. For here Christ, who has fully embraced our humanity in the mystery of the incarnation, does not retreat from the violence unleashed against the world's scapegoats and victims, but stands in their midst as one of their own. Nor does he seek to avoid, divert, or overwhelm this violence with some divine power or might. He does not flee as some have begged him to do. He does not take up Peter's sword or call down legions of angels to destroy his enemies. Instead, he walks unarmed into the heart of human violence, standing in solidarity with all other victims and scapegoats, and responding to the murderous rage of his attackers with compassion and forgiveness.

Unjustly accused, condemned, beaten, abandoned, humiliated, and executed, Christ joins humanity's endless parade of the "disappeared," tortured, and crucified. And in that same moment he refuses to be consumed by the hatred and violence that is forever harvesting new crops of scapegoats and victims, praying instead for the forgiveness for his persecutors, and for all who scapegoat and sacrifice. Not satisfying the blood lust of a wrathful god, but expressing our God's immeasurable love for all scapegoats and victims—and scandalous forgiveness of all scapegoaters and victimizers, Christ has "identified himself as victim with all the other victims."[31] Indeed, as we will see below, he has become *the* victim of our violence by being the martyr (witness) to God's love.

As Girard and others note, the God revealed in the Scriptures is not a God who demands or accepts scapegoats offered on an altar of sacrifice. Instead, this God sides with scapegoats and has become one with all sacrificial victims. In Scripture, the lie and violence of scapegoating and sacrifice have been exposed and we have been introduced to a God who stands with victims and liberates them. And God calls us to do the same. Indeed, as Gil Bailie argues, the Bible not only rejects the myth of sacrifice but has transformed the moral landscape by putting victims not last but first. Biblical revelation has turned the moral universe upside down by making victims and scapegoats the starting point of all our moral reflections and identifying compassion for these victims as our highest virtue.[32]

The Un-Sacrifice of Christ

So, if the God revealed to us in Scripture is not a God who demands or accepts sacrifices and scapegoats, what does it mean to speak about the cross or the Eucharist as a "sacrifice"? If the God of the Bible resists scapegoating, sides with scapegoats and victims, and even becomes a scapegoat to unmask and end the violence of scapegoating, how can we speak of Christ's passion and death, or of the Eucharist that memorializes this mystery, as "sacrifice"?

Certainly the "sacrifice" of the cross or the Eucharist cannot be a sacrifice like anything Girard has in mind when describing this practice, like what ancient religions and modern societies do when they seek to purchase peace by scapegoating innocent parties. Nor can it simply be a better or more perfect type of such sacrifice, for on the cross and in the Eucharist Christ is *not* merely improving on or even transcending the sacrifices offered by others. He is *not* seeking to appease the wrath or satisfy the justice of God, or to secure God's forgiveness and the community's peace by offering up a scapegoat.[33] Instead, the cross and the Eucharist are the very opposite of what we normally mean by sacrifice, for they unmask the violence and injustice of sacrifice and reveal a God of immeasurable mercy and compassion. They are, in a very real sense, the antithesis of sacrifice, witnessing to a God who is the polar opposite of wrathful deities that can or must be appeased by such offerings. Indeed, it would be better to speak of the cross and Eucharist as Christ's "un-sacrifice," for they testify to a God who rejects sacrifice and makes an end of scapegoating.[34]

The Metaphor of Sacrifice

In his work on *The Origins of the Christian Doctrine of Sacrifice,* Robert Daly acknowledges that the Old Testament reveals a God who accepts burnt offerings and holocausts. But increasingly the only "sacrifices" acceptable to this God are ones offered by those who "live up to the covenantal demands of justice and mercy."[35] The God of the Hebrews is not pleased with cultic offerings from those who oppress and cheat widows, orphans, and strangers, but God seeks a deeper, truer "sacrifice."

The "real" sacrifice desired by this God is a converted heart, a heart fully committed to imitate God's own mercy and compassion to the poor and outcasts. As Micah 6:7-8 notes, the "sacrifice" our God requires is not "thousands of rams, with ten thousands of rivers of oil" but rather "to do justice, and to love kindness, and to walk humbly with your God." Within the Old Testament, then, "sacrifice" becomes a metaphor for an obedient and loving heart, indicating that whatever reconciliation or atonement worshipers hoped to achieve through burnt offerings placed on altars could only be secured by lives spent in obedience to God and showing mercy and justice to the poor. More and more in the Bible the language of cultic offering is used to describe the complete gift of the self to God and neighbor, meaning that the "sacrifice" required by our God is not at all like the sacrifices being offered to other deities but something quite different.

Daly and David Power note that the early Christian community also used the language or metaphor of sacrifice to describe a very different kind of offering than the ones being brought to the altars and shrines of Greek and Roman deities.[36] These early Christians described both the mystery of Christ's death and resurrection and the Eucharist as "sacrifice," but they used the term metaphorically, even ironically, and did not mean that Christ's pasch and the Eucharist were anything like the burnt offerings and blood rites being offered to other gods. As Power notes, the cross and the Eucharist could be called sacrifice "because they realized superabundantly the end and purpose of sacrifice," which was to reconcile God and humanity. But they did this in a way that turned the notion of sacrifice on its head.[37]

For in the "sacrifice" of the cross and the Eucharist, humans do not reach out to appease a wrathful God with an act of violence. Instead, a merciful and nonviolent God reaches out in compassion and forgiveness to a violent and estranged humanity. In this "sacrifice" the violence of scapegoating is not sanctioned as necessary for our reconciliation with God or one another, but exposed as folly and rejected by a God who defends all scapegoats and victims, and forgives all victimizers. In this "sacrifice" an innocent victim is not slain to satisfy the justice of God. Instead, in his life, death, and resurrection Christ testifies to God's unbounded mercy by preaching and practicing a gospel of forgiveness and reconciliation, even at the cost of his own life. Christ's "sacrifice" offers humanity reconciliation with God, and does this in a way that "renders absurd and obsolete any further offering of sacrifice."[38]

Nor did the early Christian community understand Christ's "sacrifice" or Christians' participation in this offering in the Eucharist or their daily lives as a ritual act involving burnt offerings or blood rites. Rather, Christ's "sacrifice" was the total gift of his life to God and neighbor, and his disciples joined in this "sacrifice" not by offering gifts on the altar, but by following Christ's lead—leading lives of obedience to God and loving service to their neighbors.[39]

Christ's "sacrifice" does not reconcile humanity to God by scapegoating some portion of the human community, by attempting to run away from the broken, frail, or despised parts of our humanity, which is what sacrifices have always done. And Christ does not become our "priest" by separating himself out from the human community, by being lifted up above our broken humanity as one who is clean, perfect, and divine. Instead, Christ's "sacrifice" reconciles humanity to God by taking on our humanity, by embracing our frailty, and by completely immersing himself in our mortality and dependence on God.[40]

If the sin of humanity has been to "grasp at equality with God" and to try to flee from our frail human condition by climbing on the backs of a mountain of sacrificial victims and scapegoats, then Christ's "sacrifice" is the complete reversal of this sin. For in the incarnation, the God whose infinite power and perfection we envy and covet has freely and scandalously taken on the frail, imperfect, and mortal flesh we have so vainly tried to escape. And in his life and sufferings Christ has reached out to embrace the very parts of that flesh that remind us so painfully of our brokenness: the poor, the outcasts, the foreigners, the lepers, the prostitutes, the tax collectors, and the sinners—victims and scapegoats of every stripe and color. Indeed, Christ does not retreat from this selfless and generous gift even when it provokes our worst violence and costs him his very life.

And the early Christians who memorialized this "sacrifice" in the Eucharist and sought to imitate it in their lives did not feel called to offer cultic or ritual sacrifices like their Greek and Roman contemporaries. Instead, they felt obliged to offer the "sacrifice" of lives spent in loving service of the poor and marginalized. For as Daly notes, the primary understanding that early Christians had of the "sacrifice" they were offering to God was not cultic or liturgical, but referred to the moral duties of mercy and justice that they had to show to their neighbors. Christians participated in the "sacrifice" of Christ by embodying Christ's "obedience and love toward God, and self-sacrificing love and service to and for the brothers and sisters."[41]

Unfortunately, over the centuries, Christianity lost its rich, metaphorical, and ethical understanding of Christ's "sacrifice" and came instead to see both the cross and the Eucharist as sacrifice in a more literal and cultic sense. Particularly since the Middle Ages, Christian thinkers have tended to understand Christ's "sacrifice" not as the antithesis of other sacrifices but as the most perfect example of this practice. As we saw earlier, this literal view suggests that human sin, which offends God, has created a debt that can only be paid by the offering of a perfect (i.e. unblemished) sacrifice. Since Christ alone is sinless and divine, his sacrificial death is required to cancel our debt and make it possible for God to forgive us.[42]

This literal and cultic understanding, which has only recently been challenged, represented a significant distortion of the mystery of Christ's death and resurrection, and of the Eucharist that memorializes this "sacrifice." Indeed, this understanding of the "sacrifice" of the cross and the Eucharist portrayed God as (at best) a righteous and exacting judge who accepts and demands sacrificial victims in payment for past offenses, not as a merciful and nonviolent God who would offer the unimaginable gift of becoming one with all the scapegoats of human violence. What's more, because it has failed to question the underlying logic of sacrifice and scapegoating, this cultic notion of sacrifice too easily justifies all sorts of sacrificial violence and scapegoating against a wide variety of victims.[43] If the scapegoating and sacrifice of Jesus is seen as necessary for the satisfaction of our debt to God, then perhaps the victimization of women and minorities and foreigners, as well as slaves and dissidents and the "disappeared," the tortured and the executed is likewise required to preserve and protect the peace, security, and stability of our society or economy. A literal understanding of Christ's sacrifice doesn't make an end of sacrifices; it makes a virtue of them. As Power and others have argued, there is a need to recover Christianity's metaphorical understanding of Christ's "sacrifice," and see once again that what we celebrate in the Eucharist would be better called the very reversal of sacrifice.[44]

Christ's "Un-sacrifice"

From what we have already noted, it should be clear that there are four reasons why we might describe Christ's "sacrifice" as an "un-sacrifice." First, even though on the surface the story of Christ's passion and death looks very much like a tale of sacrifice, involving the scapegoating and murder of an innocent man, the biblical accounts of this event are told from the victim's point of view, and they reveal the cruel injustice and violence of sacrifice. Second, in the Bible, but particularly in the life, death, and resurrection of Jesus, God is not revealed as one who demands or accepts sacrifices or scapegoats as an appeasement for sins, or the satisfaction of a debt, but as one who offers forgiveness and mercy in a surprising—even scandalous—fashion. Third, throughout the Scriptures, but especially in the preaching and practice of Jesus, we are introduced to a God who liberates and identifies with the world's scapegoats—and certainly not one who would encourage the making of more scapegoats or the offering of further sacrificial victims. And, fourth, Jesus reveals to us a God who is nonviolent and who responds to human violence with an unfathomable (to us)—and often terrifying—compassion.

In John 11:49-50 the high priest Caiaphas argues that it is sometimes "better . . . to have one man die for the people," and indeed there are numerous elements in the account of Christ's passion and death that make it seem like another myth about sacrifice. An innocent man is accused, abandoned, condemned, and executed, and his

death is seen as saving the peace of the community and (later) as reconciling humanity to God. In many ways it is hardly surprising that
so many centuries of Christians have seen Christ's "sacrifice" literally
and not metaphorically. Still, as Girard points out, what distinguishes
the account of the Gospel from other tales of sacrifice, what makes it
truly revelatory, is that it is told from the viewpoint of the victim, and
the execution of this "victim" is not seen as good, holy, or necessary,
but as a murderous and unjust expression of human violence and
sinfulness.[45] In the story of Christ's passion and death the human violence that attempts to make a scapegoat of this victim is not overlooked or sanctioned, but exposed and condemned. And the victim is
not portrayed as one whose murder reconciles humanity to God, but
as one whose selfless and nonviolent love effects this reconciliation by
exposing, repudiating, and conquering human violence.

As we have already seen, the God of the Bible is not one who demands or accepts sacrifices and scapegoats as satisfaction for offenses
committed by a sinful humanity. Indeed, again and again in the Scriptures, God is portrayed not as one who waits for humanity to repent
of its sins but as one who rushes out to sinners and offers forgiveness
and mercy that have not been asked for or earned.[46] In three of Luke's
parables: the lost sheep, the lost coin, and the lost son (chap. 15) Jesus
describes God as one who goes out looking for sinners, rescuing them,
and rejoicing when they are found—welcoming them back with a
scandalous feast and showering them with forgiveness even before
they have a chance to ask for it. So too, in his breaking bread with tax
collectors, prostitutes, and sinners of every sort, Jesus scandalizes us
by offering God's forgiveness and mercy before it has even been
asked for, and when challenged about this outrageous behavior he
reminds his audience that "Those who are well have no need of a
physician, but those who are sick; I have come to call not the righteous but sinners" (Mark 2:17).

In his parables of the reign of God, Jesus describes a recklessly extravagant host who scours the highways and byways in search of the
most worthless and unseemly guests. This is hardly a deity who will
not be able to forgive humanity until someone has first paid off the
immeasurable debt owed as a result of past sins. Instead, the God
whom Jesus reveals, like the king in Matthew's parable of the merci-
less debtor (18:23-35), is one who cancels debts and offers forgiveness
long before it is earned.

Furthermore, Christ's "sacrifice" must be the very opposite of traditional sacrifices, indeed, must be an "un-sacrifice" because the God to whom this gift is being offered is fundamentally opposed to sacrifices and scapegoating. As we have already seen, throughout the Bible but particularly in the story of Jesus, God is revealed as one who takes the side of scapegoats and victims, who comes to their rescue and demands their liberation from every form of oppression, marginalization, and violence. This God rejects the sacrifices offered on altars and demands an interior "sacrifice" expressed in lives given over to mercy and justice for the widowed, orphans, and strangers. And this God, in an act of profligate love, takes on the form of a scapegoat, and this God embraces the identity and suffering of all victims and scapegoats. Whatever we do or fail to do on behalf of all the world's victims and scapegoats we do or fail to do for our God. Christ's offering to such a God can hardly be a sacrifice that offers up victims or scapegoats. It must instead be a gift that sides with, rescues, and liberates them.

Finally, the "sacrifice" of Christ is the reversal of all sacrifices because it does not reveal a wrathful God who can be appeased by violence—or who sanctions violence against victims and scapegoats. Rather, the "sacrifice" of Christ reveals a nonviolent God who refuses to react to human violence with vengeance or sacrifice, but instead walks unarmed into the heart of the violent mob offering only a turned cheek and unsolicited forgiveness. Christ's "sacrifice" is to be found in the witness (*martyr* means *witness*) he gives to God's limitless love and forgiveness, to a compassion that embraces the suffering of victims and resists their oppression without demonizing their victimizers.[47] At the very center of the "sacrifice" of Christ is a refusal to take up arms against his enemies and a prayer for the forgiveness of his executioners. This is hardly a God who sanctions violence.

A Remembrance of Christ's Un-Sacrifice

Given everything we have said about sacrifice and about the "un-sacrifice" of Christ, we come back to our original question about the Eucharist and sacrifice. What does it mean for us to speak about the Eucharist as a sacrifice? And in what way can this sacrifice be seen as a sacrament of peace and reconciliation? Certainly we can begin by saying that the Eucharist is a sacrifice unlike any other. Not just better or more perfect than other sacrifices, but the Eucharist is the reversal and repudiation of all sacrifices. As David Power puts it, "There is no correspondence in reality or concept between the many rites of offering known to religions and the death of Christ, or between these same and the Eucharist."[48] William Cavanaugh unpacks the difference, even opposition, between Eucharist and sacrifice in *Torture and Eucharist,* where he argues that

> Eucharistic sacrifice is the end of the violent sacrifice on which the religions of the world are based, for its aim is not to create new victims but rather martyrs, witnesses to the end of victimization. Assimilation to Christ's sacrifice is not the continuation of the violence and rivalry needed to sustain a certain conception of society, but the gathering of a new social body in which the only sacrifice is the mutual self-offering of Christian charity. Martyrs offer their lives in the knowledge that their refusal to return violence for violence is an identification with Christ's risen body and an anticipation of the heavenly banquet.[49]

As a participation in Christ's "un sacrifice," the Eucharist is most certainly not an offering meant to appease or satisfy a wrathful deity, nor does it involve or sanction the scapegoating of sacrificial victims. Christ's peace is not purchased by fragmenting the community into victimizers and victims, accusers and scapegoats. Instead, in the Eucharist we participate in the selfless and generous gift of Christ's life, a gift offered in obedience to God and love of the neighbor, and we share in the reconciliation and peace secured by this extravagant testimony to the nonviolent and merciful love of God. In the Eucharist we join ourselves to the one who sides and identifies with all victims and scapegoats, who exposes, confronts, and resists all forms of victimization and scapegoating, and who offers forgiveness to victimizers and scapegoaters. And in joining in this selfless, nonviolent, and loving "un-sacrifice" we participate in an offering that reconciles humanity to God and humans to their neighbors.

Sacrificial Amnesia

As we noted earlier, the practice of sacrifice or scapegoating depends on our forgetting a number of things. Girard argues that ancient religions could only use sacrifice to solve the double threat of violence if people were willing to forget or ignore the fact that the hostilities and rivalries simmering beneath the surface in every human society and threatening to boil over into community-destroying violence were rooted in every heart and not just in the victims and scapegoats chosen for sacrifice.[50] He also notes that sacrifices only worked if communities could forget that they were not offering these victims to appease divine wrath and they could do offer sacrifice to satisfy human vengeance. And, finally, accusers and scapegoaters could only feel good about their violence against victims if they forgot that these victims were like themselves.

At the very heart of all violence is the lie that those we accuse, attack, condemn, or kill are "not like us." And so sacrifice and scapegoating must always begin with the forgetting of what we share with those we want to blame or slay. Adam gives us the first example of this forgetting. Somewhere between Genesis 2:23 and 3:12 our ancestor conveniently forgets that "The woman whom you gave to be with me" (3:12) "is bone of my bones and flesh of my flesh" (2:23). And in the next chapter Cain has suddenly forgotten that he is his "brother's keeper" (4:9). The Pharaoh in Exodus 1:8 needed to forget about Joseph before he could set out scapegoating the Israelites. The Hebrews needed to forget their own history as slaves and refugees if they were going to oppress the resident alien who had settled in their land. And Christians have had to forget the "common spiritual heritage" they share with Jews, or they would never have been able to justify nearly two millennia of persecution and scapegoating.[51] Similarly, a patriarchal Christianity has had to forget that women are morally, intellectually, and spiritually equal to men—or they could never have allowed thousands of years of abuse, oppression, and violence.

The practice of sacrifice and scapegoating has always depended on our forgetting the humanity of our victims. We could only tolerate perpetrating this sort of violence if we convinced ourselves that these people were not like us, if we demonized them and told ourselves lies about them. The Crusades, the Inquisition, the wars of religion, the enslavement of Africans, the decimation of Native Americans, and the Holocaust—not to mention segregation, apartheid, ethnic cleansing in the Balkans, and genocide in Rwanda. None of these horrors would have been possible without first forgetting that all of these victims were bone from our bones, and flesh from our flesh.

Scapegoating and sacrifices have also depended on our forgetting our own broken humanity, ignoring our shared responsibility for all the rivalries and hostilities tearing at the fabric of every human community, and overlooking our own contributions to the ever escalating cycle of vengeance and violence threatening to overwhelm human communities. The myth of sacrifice can only be sustained by the lie of our own innocence. The self-righteous indignation we experience when blaming and scapegoating our enemies and victims requires that we turn a blind eye to our own part in the troubles and violence around us. We tar and feather our scapegoats and whitewash ourselves with the same brush. Like the mob ready to stone the woman caught in adultery in John 8:7, our desire to scapegoat is always being abetted by a convenient amnesia regarding our own complicity and sinfulness. Are there really any in our midst without sin? The splinter in our victim's eye is enormous. The plank in our own is invisible (see Luke 6:42).

And, of course, scapegoating and sacrifice only work if we forget what we are really doing here, and convince ourselves of the lie that we are seeking to appease a wrathful God. The trick of sacrifice only works if we forget that the God of the Bible is one who neither demands nor accepts scapegoats and that this offering is really intended to satisfy our own lust for vengeance or to secure that illusory peace of a mob closing in on its prey.

A Dangerous Memory

If sacrifice and scapegoating are about forgetting, then the Eucharist is about remembering. Indeed, the Eucharist is about keeping alive a dangerous and subversive memory that unveils the violence of sacrifice and scapegoating and ties us to the suffering and oppression of all the world's victims and scapegoats. In the earliest account of the Last Supper (1 Cor 11:23-26) Jesus instructs his disciples to "do this in *memory* of me" (see 1 Cor 11:23-26, words from the Sacramentary; NRSV: "Do this in remembrance of me"), and the Eucharist is a remembrance or *anamnesis* (memorial) of Christ's sacrifice.[52]

Naming the Eucharist a remembrance or memorial, however, does not mean that we are merely recalling or ritually reenacting Christ's sacrifice. It means instead that we are joining in the "un-sacrifice" of the one who stands with and liberates scapegoats by *re-membering* ourselves to the suffering Body of Christ, a body that includes all the victimized, despised, tortured, and scapegoated with whom Christ identified. As Cavanaugh notes, "The body of Christ is the suffering body, the destitute body, the body which is tortured and sacrificed. The Church is the body of Christ because it performs an *anamnesis* of Christ's sacrifice, suffering in its own flesh the afflictions taken on by Christ." And so the Eucharist "is a literal re-membering of Christ's body, a knitting together of the body of Christ by the participation of many in His sacrifice."[53] In the Eucharist we are re-membering ourselves to the suffering Body of Christ and to the bodies of all the suffering and sacrificed.

In the Eucharist we re-member ourselves (or perhaps it would be better to say that Christ re-members us) to the sacrifice of the one who could not forget the suffering of scapegoats and victims. In the Eucharist we realize our identity as Church and as the Body of Christ by re-membering ourselves to the one who would not scapegoat or sacrifice others—the Body of Christ who stands with and liberates victims and scapegoats, and the Body of Christ who exposes, confronts, and resists all forms of victimization and violence. In this *anamnesis,* this "dangerous memory" as the German theologian Johann-Baptist Metz describes it, we are stripped of our sacrificial amnesia and we remember the scandalous suffering and nonviolent love of our God, a God who takes on our frail and broken flesh and embraces all victims and scapegoats, a God who walks defenselessly into the heart of human violence and absorbs and conquers this violence with love. Christianity is, as Metz notes, a "community of memory," a community grounded in and nurtured by the *memoria passionis, mortis et resurrectionis Jesu Christi* (the memory of Christ's passion, death, and resurrection), and this memory or remembrance joins us to that sacrifice and calls us to live and love as a people who cannot forget the suffering of others.[54]

And in re-membering ourselves to Christ's sacrifice, we also re-member ourselves to all those whom Christ could not forget. In the *anamnesis* of Christ's passion, death, and resurrection, we remember the sufferings of all victims and scapegoats, of all the despised, tortured, and "disappeared." For the Christ we remember and join ourselves to in the Eucharist has already identified with all the hungry, homeless, sick, imprisoned, and dying (Matt 25:31-46). And so in this *anamnesis* the joys and hopes and fears and anxieties of all the afflicted and poor are now *our* joys and hopes and fears and anxieties.[55]

This *anamnesis* of Christ's sacrifice is a "dangerous memory" because in re-membering us to the suffering Body of Christ and the suffering bodies of all victims and scapegoats, the Eucharist unmasks the violence and injustice embedded in our communities, a hidden and structural violence that is forever manufacturing new victims and scapegoats. The dangerous memory of the Eucharist uncovers this violence as unjust and unjustified, as needing to be reformed. The subversive memory of the Eucharist, which will not forget the sufferings of those pushed off to the margins or accept the "official version" of history that attends only to the victors and the successful, unmasks the violence of our communities and contrasts it with the "future memory" of God's coming reign. In the beggars' banquet of the Eucharist we remember the perspective of all the victims and scapegoats who are being given the places of honor at the heavenly banquet. In the *anamnesis* of the Eucharist we remember that "the way things are" is not "the way things have to be"—or are meant to be. In the Eucharist we remember our eschatological hope of a community where there are no victimizers and victims, scapegoaters and scapegoated, torturers and tortured.

At the same time, the *anamnesis* of the Eucharist is a dangerous and disturbing memory because it uncovers our own share and participation in the victimization and scapegoating of others. In the remembrance of the suffering of the Body of Christ we are also reminded of our own violence and sinfulness, of our own failure to remember the humanity of our neighbors. The *memoria passionis* at the heart of the Eucharist uncovers both the sufferings and victimization of others— and our own support or tolerance of that victimization. In the *anamnesis* of the Eucharist we remember that we are not simply innocent bystanders, that our brothers and sisters have complaints against *us,* and that we need to repent and be reconciled before bringing our gift to the altar (see Matt 5:23-24).

For those of us who lead fairly comfortable lives the *anamnesis* of the Eucharist is a subversive memory about the ways the poor and dispossessed have been sacrificed to secure our daily bread, our standard of living, or our national security. As Enrique Dussel argues, in the Eucharist we remember that "God cannot accept bread that is stolen from the poor, the bread of injustice."[56] In the Eucharist we remember that "If one sacrifices from ill-gotten goods, the offering is blemished; the gifts of the lawless are not acceptable. . . . Like one who kills a son before his father's eyes is the person who offers a sacrifice from the property of the poor" (Sir 34:21-24).

And the *anamnesis* of the Eucharist is a dangerous memory because it offers victims and scapegoats a way to name and claim their own experience of suffering, and to find in Christ's "un-sacrifice" a witness on behalf of a loving and nonviolent God who sides and identifies with them, a God who refuses to accept the violence perpetrated against them as a sacrificial offering, but who exposes, confronts, and resists their victimization and oppression. In the *anamnesis* of the Eucharist we remember the violence directed against the suffering Body of Christ as unjust, and in so doing we recognize the victimization and scapegoating of all peoples as having nothing to do with the God to whom we offer praise and thanksgiving in this sacrament.

In the *anamnesis* of the Eucharist the passion, death, and resurrection of Christ has rescued all victims and scapegoats from their invisibility and enforced silence, and rendered them "un-disappeared," placing their experiences, stories, and perspective front and center in the Christian memory. As Bailie argues, victims and scapegoats have now become the moral center of our universe and compassion for these little ones our central moral virtue.[57]

In the remembrance of the Eucharist, the world's victims and scapegoats are empowered to remember their own experience as crucified and to find in Jesus one who stands with and loves them. As R. Kevin Seasoltz notes, there are countless numbers among us who are more sinned against than sinners. So many of the world's women, of "the poor, the unemployed, the redundant, the manipulated, and the racially, religiously and sexually marginalized . . . live in the underside of history."[58] And the *anamnesis* of the Eucharist remembers their suffering, uncovers their victimization, and brings them first and foremost the Good News of God's love and promise of liberation.

As wounded victims contemplating Jesus as the innocent victim on the cross they can be helped to discover themselves not primarily as crucifiers of a sinless victim but as victims themselves who have been wounded and slain by the injustices of the world. Hence Jesus becomes, as the crucified victim, an ally; God the Father becomes a grieving parent; and the risen Lord Jesus becomes the one who offers both healing and empowerment through the gift of the Spirit.[59]

The *anamnesis* of the Eucharist also resists any further victimizing or scapegoating of persons that would have them take on or overlook the sins of their victimizers. All too often an incomplete gospel of repentance and forgiveness has been preached to both victims and victimizers in a way that ignored the differences between them and pressed victims to take the blame for their victimization and/or shower their unrepentant victimizers with forgiveness.[60] This combination of "guilt tripping" and "cheap grace" has not brought about genuine reconciliation but is simply a further scapegoating of sacrificial victims. Any real "remembrance" of Christ's sacrifice must re-member us to the suffering bodies of victims and scapegoats in ways that allow us to recognize and resist their victimization. As Gustavo Gutierrez notes, "Without a real commitment against exploitation and alienation and for a society of solidarity and justice, the Eucharistic celebration is an empty action."[61]

This does not mean that the *anamnesis* of the Eucharist does not re-member the humanity of victimizers and scapegoaters. For the Christ whose passion, death, and resurrection we remember in the Eucharist pleads for the forgiveness of his victimizers and scapegoaters—and thus for all of us who participate in and benefit from these processes. But God's incredible offer of forgiveness and Christ's nonviolent love for those of us who victimize and scapegoat does not cancel the fact that God sides with victims and scapegoats, and God exposes, confronts, and resists every sort of victimization and scapegoating. In the Eucharist we re-member ourselves to the suffering Body of Christ, a body that stands and identifies with victims, a body that makes a preferential option for scapegoats—and that calls victimizers and scapegoaters to repentance and reconciliation.

Finally, the *anamnesis* of the Eucharist remembers the humanity and the suffering of our enemies. In the Eucharist we remember that the one we have despised and hated is bone from our bones and flesh from our flesh (see Gen 2:23). In the Eucharist we remember that "[t]here is no longer Jew or Greek, there is no longer slave or free, there is no longer male and female; for all of [us] are one in Christ Jesus" (Gal 3:28). And we remember that we are to love our enemies and pray for those who persecute us (see Matt 5:44). These are disturbing memories indeed.

Conclusion

In the Eucharist we participate in the sacrifice of Christ, a holy and perfect sacrifice "which has made our peace" with God and which "advance[s] the peace and the salvation of all the world."[62] But this "sacrifice" is unlike any other ever offered, and the peace that it bears is unlike anything the world has ever known. For Christ's sacrifice (or "un-sacrifice") does not seek to appease a wrathful God or secure peace through the victimization or scapegoating of sacrificial offerings. Instead, it exposes, confronts, and resists every form of sacrifice and scapegoating, siding and identifying with victims and scapegoats—and refusing to make new victims or scapegoats through sacrifice or vengeance. Indeed, this sacrifice gives witness to a God who does not demand or accept sacrifices, but offers and expects mercy and compassion—a God whose scandalous and nonviolent love absorbs and conquers every sort of human violence. In the Eucharist we participate in Christ's sacrifice by being re-membered to the suffering Body of Christ and thus to all the suffering bodies with whom Christ has been identified. And in this *anamnesis* we are called to live our lives in "remembrance" of the one who sided with scapegoats and liberated victims.

Notes

[1] *Baltimore Catechism No. 2,* q. 263.

[2] Council of Trent (1562): *Doctrina de ss. Missae sacrificio,* chap. 2 in Denziger and Schönmetzer, no. 1743, cited in *The Catechism of the Catholic Church,* 2d ed. (Washington, D.C.: U.S. Catholic Conference, 1997) no. 1367.

[3] R. Kevin Seasoltz, "Human Victimization and Christ as Victim in the Eucharist," *Worship* 76 (2002) 106–7.

[4] *Catechism of the Catholic Church,* no. 1367.

[5] For a discussion of the recovery of meal imagery, see Philippe Rouillard, "From Human Meal to Christian Eucharist," part 2, *Worship* 53 (1979) 44–54.

[6] James Williams, *The Bible, Violence and the Sacred: Liberation from the Myth of Sanctioned Violence* (Valley Forge, Pa.: Trinity Press International, 1995) 14–20; see also David Power, "Words That Crack: The Uses of 'Sacrifice' in Eucharistic Discourse," *Worship* 53 (1979) 399–402.

[7] David Power, *The Eucharistic Mystery: Revitalizing the Tradition* (New York: Crossroad, 1995) 322.

[8] René Girard, *Violence and the Sacred,* trans. Patrick Gregory (Baltimore, Md.: Johns Hopkins University, 1977).

[9] See Louis-Marie Chauvet, *Symbol and Sacrament: A Sacramental Reinterpretation of Christian Existence* (Collegeville: The Liturgical Press, 1995) 303–6; see also Williams, *The Bible, Violence and the Sacred,* 6–14.

[10] Girard, *Violence and the Sacred,* 7.

[11] Gil Bailie, *Violence Unveiled: Humanity at the Crossroads* (New York: Crossroad, 1997) 218–23; see James Carroll, *Constantine's Sword: The Church and the Jews: A History* (New York: Houghton Mifflin, 2001).

[12] The International Theological Commission, "Memory and Reconciliation: The Church and the Faults of the Past," *Origins,* 16 March 2000, 625–44; see nos. 81–87.

[13] Bishop Jorge Mejia, "The Roots of Violence Against Women," *Origins,* 4 November 1993, 369.

[14] Elizabeth Schüssler Fiorenza and Mary Shawn Copeland, eds., *Violence Against Women,* Concilium, 1994/1 (Maryknoll, N.Y.: Orbis, 1994) x–xvii. See also Catholic Church, Assemblée des évêques du Québec, Comité épiscopal des affaires sociales, *A Heritage of Violence?: A Pastoral Reflection on Conjugal Violence,* trans. Antoinette Kinlough (Montréal: Social Affairs Committee of the Assembly of Quebec Bishops, 1990).

[15] For a discussion of social attitudes towards single mothers, see Thomas Massaro, *Catholic Social Teaching and the United States Welfare Reform* (Collegeville: The Liturgical Press, 1998) 73–75.

[16] Gordon Allport, *The Nature of Prejudice* (Cambridge, Mass.: Addison Wesley, 1954).

[17] Patricia Beattie Jung and Ralph F. Smith, *Heterosexism: An Ethical Challenge* (New York: SUNY Press, 1993) 90–99.

[18] Elliott Currie, *Crime and Punishment in America* (New York: Metropolitan, 1998) 32–33; see also Herbert J. Gans, *The War Against the Poor: The Underclass and Antipoverty Policy* (New York: HarperCollins, 1995); and Ruth Sidel, *Keeping Women and Children Last: America's War on the Poor* (New York: Penguin, 1996).

[19] *The Real War on Crime: The Report of the National Criminal Justice Commission,* ed. Steven Donziger (New York: HarperCollins, 1996) 29.

[20] Patrick T. McCormick, "Just Punishment and America's Prison Experiment," *Theological Studies* 61 (2000) 508–32.

[21] David Musto, *The American Disease: Origins of Narcotic Control,* rev. ed. (New York: Oxford University, 1987); see also John Helmer, *Drugs and Minority Oppression* (New York: Seabury Press, 1975).

[22] Michael Tonry, *Malign Neglect: Race, Crime and Punishment in America* (New York: Oxford University, 1995) 97, 101–10; see also Mark Mauer, *Race to Incarcerate* (New York: New Press, 1999) 143–51.

[23] Eric Schlosser, "The Prison-Industrial Complex," *Atlantic Monthly* (December 1998) 54.

[24] Rene Girard, *Things Hidden Since the Foundation of the World* (Stanford: Stanford University Press, 1987); see also Chauvet, *Symbol and Sacrament,* 303–6; Power, *The Eucharistic Mystery,* 320–24; Raymond Schwager, "Christ's Death and the Prophetic Critique of Sacrifice," *Semeia* 33 (1985) 109–23; Williams, *The Bible, Violence and the Sacred,* 213–40.

[25] Bailie, *Violence Unveiled,* 44–45, 114, 133–37.

[26] Chauvet, *Symbol and Sacrament,* 303.

[27] Bailie, *Violence Unveiled,* 141.

[28] See above, chap. 3, note 1.

[29] See Williams, *The Bible, Violence, and the Sacred,* 148–62; Bailie, *Violence Unveiled,* 167–84.

[30] Bailie, *Violence Unveiled,* 212–16.

[31] Schwager, "Christ's Death and the Prophetic Critique of Sacrifice," 118; Bailie, *Violence Unveiled,* 217.

[32] Bailie, *Violence Unveiled,* 20–29.

[33] Power, *Eucharistic Mystery,* 322; Power, "Words that Crack," 389.

[34] Chauvet calls the sacrifice of Christ an "anti-sacrifice" in *Symbol and Sacrament,* 302; for another description of the difference between Christ's sacrifice and expiation or satisfaction, see Anthony Gittins, "Sacrifice, Violence, and the Eucharist," *Worship* 65 (1991) 420–22.

[35] Robert J. Daly, *The Origins of the Christian Doctrine of Sacrifice* (Philadelphia: Fortress, 1978) 136–37.

[36] Power, *Eucharistic Mystery,* 320–24; Power, "Words That Crack," 386–404; Daly, *The Origins of the Christian Doctrine of Sacrifice,* 137–40.

[37] Power, *Eucharistic Mystery,* 321.

[38] Power, "Words That Crack," 387.

[39] Daly, *The Origins of the Christian Doctrine of Sacrifice,* 137–38.

[40] Chauvet, *Symbol and Sacrament,* 299–302.

[41] Daly, *The Origins of the Christian Doctrine of Sacrifice,* 138.

[42] Power, *Eucharistic Mystery,* 321–22; Seasoltz, "Human Victimization and Christ as Victim in the Eucharist," 106–8.

[43] Power, *Eucharistic Mystery,* 320; Seasoltz, "Human Victimization and Christ as Victim in the Eucharist," 110–19.

[44] Power, *Eucharistic Mystery,* 322–23.

[45] See Bailie, *Violence Unveiled,* 129; Girard, *Things Hidden Since the Foundation of the World,* 167–70, 180–85.

[46] Schwager, "Christ's Death and the Prophetic Critique of Sacrifice," 111–13.

[47] Gittins, "Sacrifice, Violence, and the Eucharist," 430–32.

[48] Power, "Words That Crack," 389.

[49] William T. Cavanaugh, *Torture and Eucharist: Theology, Politics and the Body of Christ* (Malden, Mass.: Blackwell, 1998) 232.

[50] Girard, *Violence and the Sacred,* 82–83.

[51] The bishops of Vatican II acknowledged this common heritage and the part of the debt Christianity owes to Judaism in *Nostra Aetate* (Declaration on the Relation of the Church to Non-Christian Religions) no. 4, in *Vatican Council II: The Conciliar and Post Conciliar Documents,* ed. Austin Flannery (Boston: St. Paul Editions, 1981) 740–41.

[52] Gittins, "Sacrifice, Violence, and the Eucharist," 423.

[53] Cavanaugh, *Torture and Eucharist,* 229.

⁵⁴ See Johann-Baptist Metz, *Love's Strategy: The Political Theology of Johann Baptist Metz,* ed. John K. Downey (Harrisburg, Pa.: Trinity, 1999) 169–74; Johann Baptist Metz and Jürgen Moltmann, *Faith and the Future: Essays on Theology, Solidarity and Modernity* (Maryknoll, N.Y.: Orbis, 1995) 10–13.

⁵⁵ See *Gaudium et Spes* (Pastoral Constitution on the Church in the Modern World) in *Catholic Social Thought: The Documentary Heritage,* ed. David J. O'Brien and Thomas A. Shannon (Maryknoll, N.Y.: Orbis, 1992) 166.

⁵⁶ Enrique Dussel, "The Bread of the Eucharistic Celebration as a Sign of Justice in the Community," in *Can We Always Celebrate the Eucharist?* ed. Mary Collins and David Power, Concilium (New York), 152 (New York: Seabury Press, 1982) 63.

⁵⁷ Bailie, *Violence Unveiled,* 20–29.

⁵⁸ Seasoltz, "Human Victimization and Christ as Victim in the Eucharist," 113.

⁵⁹ Ibid.

⁶⁰ Christine Gudorf, *Victimization: Examining Christian Complicity* (Philadelphia: Trinity, 1992) 75–93.

⁶¹ Gustavo Gutierrez, *A Theology of Liberation* (Maryknoll, N.Y.: Orbis, 1973) 265.

⁶² See Eucharistic Prayer III in the current Sacramentary.